THE
UPSIDE
OF OIL AND GAS
INVESTING

THE
UPSIDE
OF OIL AND GAS
INVESTING

How the New Model Works
AND WHY IT PUTS THE TRADITIONAL MODEL TO SHAME

JAY R. YOUNG

ForbesBooks

Published by ForbesBooks, Charleston, South Carolina.
Member of Advantage Media Group.

ForbesBooks is a registered trademark, and the ForbesBooks colophon is a trademark of Forbes Media, LLC.

Printed in the United States of America.

10 9 8 7 6 5 4 3

ISBN: 978-1-94-663366-8
LCCN: 2019937168

Book design by Melanie Cloth.

This publication is designed to provide accurate and authoritative information in regard to the subject matter covered. It is sold with the understanding that the publisher is not engaged in rendering legal, accounting, or other professional services. If legal advice or other expert assistance is required, the services of a competent professional person should be sought.

Advantage Media Group is proud to be a part of the Tree Neutral® program. Tree Neutral offsets the number of trees consumed in the production and printing of this book by taking proactive steps such as planting trees in direct proportion to the number of trees used to print books. To learn more about Tree Neutral, please visit **www.treeneutral.com**.

Since 1917, the Forbes mission has remained constant. Global Champions of Entrepreneurial Capitalism. ForbesBooks exists to further that aim by bringing the Stories, Passion, and Knowledge of top thought leaders to the forefront. ForbesBooks brings you The Best in Business. To be considered for publication, please visit **www.forbesbooks.com**.

I could not have gone down the path of writing a book without the support of my wife, family, and employees. This book is for the investor, in the hope that they will come to recognize a good oil and gas deal whereby they have the potential of truly making money in this extraordinary business.

CONTENTS

DISCLAIMER

This book is intended to provide members of the public with educational information about oil and gas, oil and gas investing, and King Operating Corporation. Nothing in this book is to be construed as an offer to sell, or a solicitation of an offer to buy any security or investment product. Investments in oil and gas products offered by King Operating Corporation or any affiliate thereof are only made through Confidential Private Placement Memorandum and only to accredited investors, as defined in under the Securities Act of 1933. Investments in oil and natural gas products are speculative and involve a high degree of risk. Oil and natural gas wells are naturally depleting assets. Cash flows and returns may vary and are not guaranteed. Past performance is no indication of future performance. Nothing herein shall be construed as tax, accounting, or legal advice. The opinions offered in this book are solely those of the author unless indicated otherwise. Although the author has made every effort to ensure that the information in this book was correct at press time, the author does not assume, and hereby expressly disclaims, any liability to any party for any loss, damage, or disruption caused by errors or omissions, whether such errors or omissions result from negligence, accident, or other cause. Please consult your own legal, financial, and accounting advisors before pursuing any of the investment strategies discussed in this book.

ABOUT THE AUTHOR

Jay Young has a lifelong passion for the oil and gas business, and his family. His family has been in the business for over one hundred years. His affinity for the oil patch led Mr. Young to found King Operating Corporation.

King's business model is designed to minimize risk by acquiring and developing areas with a long history of producing oil and gas. Jay and his associates developed a unique method for the oil and gas business to acquire scalable assets in a proven field, utilize equity to start, and debt to prove up the field and divest to a larger company. When he is not busy developing oil and gas projects, Jay hosts his own weekly podcast, The Jay Young Show. Ever fond of the broadcast booth, Jay enjoys conducting personal interviews with a wide variety of guests, including CEOs, entrepreneurs, authors, athletes, and veterans.

Complimenting his professional endeavors, his wife, Michelle, and four daughters represent focal points in his life pursuits. An avid

Texas Rangers fan and former partial owner, Jay has fond memories of the MLB team's run for the World Series in 2010 and 2011.

Additionally, Jay enjoys participating in local and national philanthropic organizations such as serving on the Executive Board of Directors for Circle Ten Council (Boy Scouts of America), the North Central Texas Alzheimer's Association, and the Foundation Board of his alma mater, Angelo State University, where he graduated with a BBA degree.

ACKNOWLEDGEMENTS

No matter how you look at it, writing a book is a daunting prospect. It takes dedication, hard work, and most of all, time. As such, no one ever truly writes a book alone. To that end, I want to thank the people who helped me along the way and made this book possible.

First, my family. My wonderful and patient wife, who is my true partner in every sense of the word, and my four daughters. You have given me the time and space to put my thoughts into words and have given this old oil and gas man more joy than I could have ever hoped for.

To my parents, who showed me how to make my way in the world and how to embrace putting in a hard day's work. I am truly a better person because of the example you set for me.

To my mentors, many of whom are not even aware of the influence they've had on me: Trevor Rees-Jones, Bobby Lyle, Waring

Partridge, David Boyett, David Moore, Michael Sonnenfelt, Chris Ryan, and the entire TIGER 21 network. You have all taught me more than you know and I continually return to the well of your encouragement and inspiration.

To my King Operating team, our finance team, Rex Gifford, and former employees Stephen Perkins and Todd Garner, with their think tank on designing this particular investment for our partners; my assistant, Marcella Smith, and Bob Reilly, Brian Stubblefield, Bryan Payne, and everyone involved in the actual drilling, completing, and production of wells. And finally, to the editorial team at ForbesBooks, including Josh Houston, Amelia Arthur-Smith, and Rachel Griffin. Thank you for keeping me on track.

PREFACE

This is not where I thought I would end up. I never thought I'd be writing a book about oil and gas investments after a long and successful career in the industry. When my great-grandfather started in the oil business over one hundred years ago, he wouldn't have predicted that I would be working in this industry and certainly wouldn't have predicted that I would be writing a book about the industry. But my family can't seem to get away from oil and gas. We've been doing it for so long that it's become part of us. There have been times when it hasn't been a particularly welcome part, but it's always been there. And with that experience has come expertise and know-how. Though all the men in my family before me were laborers and not executives, I consider myself lucky to have seen their hard work up close and personal. It's helped keep me grounded and it serves to remind me of why I shouldn't take any part of this business for granted. My father, who is an extremely cautious man and who hates to put himself in the position to take risks or potentially lose money, surely wouldn't have predicted that his son would be advising people on million-dollar oil and gas investments. But what he wanted for me was a better life than he had, so at the end of the day, he can't be too surprised. My grandfather didn't want my dad to get into this business, and my dad didn't want me to get into this business because the men before them died from cirrhosis of the liver, after drinking themselves to death. The thing about the oil business is that you drink in good times, and you drink in bad times, and the oil business brings you a lot of both. But despite everyone's best intentions, this is where I ended up. Now I'm hoping I can take what I've learned and help you.

Born at the turn of the century, my great-grandfather worked himself to death. There was nothing glamorous about oil back then, at least not for the laborers like my great-grandfather. It was a hard living and only those people with strong backs and strong constitutions got involved. People were still leery of what an investment of this kind would mean for them, and those getting rich on this "Texas Tea" were not the people actually doing the work, like my great-grandfather. The people who were getting their hands dirty weren't the same ones making the money.

By the time my grandfather entered the business and spent his days (and many of his nights) out in the oil fields watching pumps and listening for the telltale sound of a malfunction, *The Beverly Hillbillies* had premiered, bringing with it unrealistic expectations of geysers of oil shooting from the ground, riches flowing in their wake. Those on the outside of the business envisioned fast wealth and endless return, all with the relatively small undertaking of drilling a hole in the ground. But as with his father before him, my grandfather understood the backbreaking work involved in drilling for oil. He knew the physical toll it could take on a person and he became an expert at taking naps for five or ten minutes at a time, sneaking in as much rest as possible wherever and whenever he could. There is no "off duty" for an oil man. My grandfather knew that better than anyone. He didn't want my father to follow in his footsteps because he knew what a hard life it could be. But as any of you who have children know, what we want for them is often beside the point. So, my dad entered the oil business as well, also as a laborer. When he was a teenager, he'd help out my grandfather and spent most of his time neck deep in empty oil tanks using high pressure salt water to clean off the accumulated scum and sediment that inevitably built up in the tank. It was dirty, hot, unpleasant work and, like his father before him, he didn't want the same for his son.

Luckily for him, my dad got what he wanted ... partly. While I don't clean oil tanks for a living, like all the men in my family before me, I can't fully get away from the industry. Instead of joining in the oil fields and working on a drilling rig, I got involved in the investment side of things, and that is where I have spent most of my career. I have seen the ups and downs of the industry and have had a front row seat to all the tax incentives, legislation, industrial accidents, sky-rocketing and plunging oil prices, and oil fortunes made and lost. I have, in short, seen it all. And while this is surely not what my great-grandfather would have predicted over a hundred years ago, I'm here now to share what I've learned with you and to help you make smarter decisions when it comes to investing in oil and gas.

One of the most important things I have learned along the way is how crucial it is to listen to others and learn what you can from them. Just because someone is in a different industry doesn't mean they don't have anything to offer. I learned that lesson on a ski lift in Beaver Creek, Colorado, and used benchmarking to establish King

Operating's new way of doing business. And it is my hope that some of the lessons learned from this book might be applicable to different lines of business as well. Just because we're talking about oil and gas here doesn't mean these same principles can't be applied to other investment opportunities.

I continue to see a lot of oil deals where investors are not given a realistic "upside." I wanted to write this book in order to explain the pitfalls and opportunities involved in oil and gas investing so that investors, like you, can make a well-educated decision when deciding whether to invest in a particular oil and gas project. We started with $37 million of equity in 2015 and our proved reserves are over $200 million as of the writing of this book. While we certainly cannot guarantee our future projects can be this successful, the investment model we are currently using, in my opinion, gives our clients a better chance to make positive returns. In contrast, the investment model for most of the oil deals with which I am familiar that are currently on the market do not give the investors the best chance to make money, and that drives me absolutely crazy. *This is the most important reason I wanted to write a book.* As you will note throughout the book, I love this business, but most of all, I want investors to have the opportunity to participate in this extraordinary investment, with a transparent understanding of both the downside risks and the upside potential. For clarity, this book is not about investing in the equity of a business, whether public or private, that is engaged in the

> *I want investors to have the opportunity to participate in this extraordinary investment, with a transparent understanding of both the downside risks and the upside potential.*

oil and gas industry (e.g., Exxon or Concho) in which the investor owns an indirect interest in all of the company's assets and operations (by virtue of owning its stock). This book is about investing in specific single or multiwell oil and gas opportunities or projects that are put together or sponsored by a company who primarily brings in third-party investors for specific oil and gas projects rather than having investors invest in the holding company and who would, by virtue of owning equity in the company, generally indirectly own an interest in all of the company's operations. In this book, I will refer to these transactions as "investment deals" or similar wording.

I hope that you will also consider this book an invitation to find out more about me, King Operating, or oil and gas investing. I am happy to talk to anyone with questions about how they can get involved. I'm a big believer in the idea of paying it forward and helping out others with what I've learned and experienced over the years and I'd be happy to help you.

Thank you for being here and let's get started.

INTRODUCTION

F irst, let me take this opportunity to thank you for reading this book. Thank you for your patience and your open-mindedness. I wouldn't have blamed you if you saw this book and pushed it aside, certain there was nothing new in here. You may assume that you've heard everything anyone would care to tell you about oil and gas investment (and you may have), and that there's nothing new to learn. So, if you did pick up this book and you're reading this now, thank you again for giving me a chance.

If you've invested in oil and gas before and you've had a bad experience—as is entirely likely—I appreciate your willingness to get on the merry-go-round again and take another spin. Although, hopefully, with my years of experience guiding the way, if you were to invest with me, you'll have an easier time of it and a much more positive experience this time around. Because I've been in the industry all my life and worked in many capacities, I've seen some good deals where people made money, and some bad deals where everything went bust. Through all of my years of experience, I have come to develop a sixth sense for when a deal seems like a bad idea from the get-go, and those that may actually have a shot at making some money for their investors. And those bad deals, unfortunately, come along a lot more often than you might think.

The truth of the matter is that the way the vast majority of oil and gas investment deals are structured means they have limited running room and little diversification. In other words, if something goes wrong—and in a complex system like drilling for oil, things can certainly go wrong—there are few ways to fix it without pouring more money into a literal hole in the ground. In these types of cases, it becomes nearly impossible for the investors to recoup their investment. Talk about "Buyer, beware!" If you're an investor, you *could* come out the other side a billionaire, but you may also be several million dollars poorer than when you went in. In the meantime, the promoter who sold the plan to you has moved on to the next big thing. In some cases, promoters make a whole lot of money on these investments whether they pan out well for the investors or not. Even worse, some promoters don't seem to care whether the investors make money on the project, as long as they got *their* paycheck.

Of course, today we all know that the industry is changing, and with threats ranging from geopolitical issues to the rise in electric vehicles and alternative fuel sources, we need repeat investors now more than ever if we're going to stay in business. If we turn people off by doing deals in which they lose money over and over, why would they ever come back to us to invest again? In the best interests of the industry and the investors, we had to start doing something differently. I knew something had to change. This book describes that change.

Even though the oil and gas industry is old and is notoriously resistant to change, I wanted to change the way we did business. Thus, I started talking to friends and acquaintances. As a member of TIGER 21, a peer network organization for high-net-worth individuals, I consulted other members, as well as people who knew something about investments, whatever their field. After what amounted to years of looking for a better way and searching for a method of managing investments that made sense both to the drilling company and to the investors, I realized the problem: generally, the industry was thinking of investors as money first rather than true partners.

In the best interests of the industry and the investors, we had to start doing something differently. I knew something had to change. This book describes that change.

After talking to a lot of people in a variety of industries and grilling them about how they did business and how they approached investors, what I came to realize is that all people really want is a genuine *shot*. People aren't even interested in a guarantee, they want to believe that they've got a shot to make a profit, or at least make their money back. That's what I knew we had to give them.

The investment model for sponsored oil and gas transactions that I discuss in this book represents a total change in the way much of the smaller, independent companies in the oil and gas industry operate. Instead of buying one location, drilling, and hoping for the best, the operator buys a lot of acreage, proves up a well, and then sells it off. And the investors can be along for the whole ride. By doing things this new way, without having to drill all the wells, projects can also be completed faster. That means there's a better opportunity for a turnaround time and for money to make it back into the investors' pockets faster. This, in turn, means another project can start, ideally with the same investors on board.

Doing things this new way essentially means that the unknown future performance of the wells is not as critical to the initial investors. In fact, by selling off the acreage to companies who want to drill, this new model has removed investors from the operation before it gets potentially dicey and goes on to something new. At the end of the day, it doesn't matter whether a well gushes or trickles; if the sponsor has been able to sell off the acreage at a higher price than the original acquisition price, the investors will have already made back their money.

The second part of this is because we want our investors to be with us for the long haul from project to project, we treat them like full business partners. We're building partnerships, not solely looking for money, and it will not surprise you to hear that when people are treated with respect, they're a whole lot more likely to reinvest with a company. As a result, we've enjoyed repeat investors for several of our most recent projects.

In oil and gas, we talk about the four Rs: returns, rate, running room, and repeatability. We have determined that if we can take care of all four of them, we've got a really good shot of paying back our investors, and then some.

Returns refer to whether or not the project makes economic sense. We have to present a plan that makes good financial sense for us to consider moving forward with a project. If it doesn't make sense, we're not going to push forward; that would be a waste of everyone's time.

Rate refers to the high rates of hydrocarbons (or oil and gas) that we can produce in a single area. This is what we mean when we talk about proving up a location. If we can get a high rate of production, it'll make it that much easier to sell the prospect.

Running room is the number of locations we're drilling in any given project. We have over one hundred locations on many projects, which makes it that much easier for us to produce a good rate. The more locations available for drilling, the more opportunities for producing a good rate—and the greater chance of investors making their money back and then some.

And finally, repeatability refers to the likelihood that we can repeat this process again and again with different acreage, ideally bringing along the same investors as business partners time and time again. If we have the first three Rs covered, we know we've got a good project on our hands.

As you read this book, you'll encounter a number of topics that will help you gain a better understanding of the oil and gas industry and the investor's role in it. First, I'll tell you a little bit about myself, my family, and our over one hundred years in the business. When I work with someone, I like to know a little bit about them. It helps me place them in context and gives me an idea of the kind of person I'm trusting with my time and money. You deserve the same thing.

Throughout this book, I'll explain the way oil and gas investments have traditionally been done, at least as far back as I can remember. I'll dissect a deal in detail, and show you the pitfalls investors can find themselves falling into when they sign onto a deal structured according to the traditional model. Then I'll explain the new way we've started doing business at King Operating and why it's been generally working so well for both us and our investors.

We'll discuss what I think is the best way to do things by examining the anatomy of a project that King Operating is involved in and how all the pieces fell into place. This deal is emblematic of most of the deals we do today, so understanding the workings of it will allow you to grasp the concept of any potential future deal that you might become a part of.

The oil and gas industry is a truly global one and, as such, it is affected by many different things that happen across the world. Everything from natural disasters to political coups to industrial accidents and trade wars can impact the price of oil. This book will explore these factors in detail, providing you with a primer on the global oil industry so that you will be better informed when it comes time for you to make your investment choices.

In addition to the external factors for a good investment, you will need to know what kind of internal relationships you need to look for in a good deal as well. With this in mind, I will also explore the concept of teamwork and the necessity of making your investors part of your team. I will explain some of the connections I've made along the way and some of the teams I have been proud to be a part of. I'll tell you what I've learned and how I strive to bring those lessons to the oil industry with me every day.

Finally, I'll look to the future of the industry. I will address some of the challenges we face from alternative fuel sources and some of the opportunities we have in emerging markets. I will also explain how you as an investor can help shape that future to ensure you have a place in it.

Once again, thank you for taking the time to pick up this book and give it a read. Thank you for putting your trust in me and for allowing me the opportunity to add you to our team. It is my sincere hope that with this knowledge on board, you can not only make informed decisions about where and how to invest your money, but that you will feel confident knowing that the company you have invested with truly cares about and respects you and has your best interests in mind. Investing in oil and gas is complicated, but if done strategically, methodically, and economically, it can be a great way to build wealth quickly. After reading this book, you'll know some of the questions to ask when you consider investing and you will be educated, prepared, and ready to become a true partner.

CHAPTER 1
A LIFETIME IN OIL AND GAS

O il is in my blood. I know the industry in my bones. There was no getting around it. I have spent my whole life around oil and gas and have come to know the industry inside and out, backwards and forwards. I know the good and the bad, the risky business and the sure thing. I have made a lot of money—but I've lost some too. And with all that experience, I have come to understand what I believe is the best way to invest in oil and gas, and the wrong way. The way I see it, the way it has been historically done is not the best way. But there is, in my opinion, a better way. There's no teacher like experience and I have experience in spades. I come from a family with over a century of experience in oil; I'm a fourth-generation oil man.

I grew up in Sulphur Springs, Texas, a town of about fifteen thousand located in the northeast corner of the state roughly eighty miles east of Dallas. But I was not the first in my family to embark on a life in oil and gas. Before me, three previous generations made their living working the oil fields and grinding out a life in the flat, open plains of Texas that seem to go on forever. Recently, I met someone at a trade show who asked where I was from. When I told him, he looked at me, drew in his breath, and said, "That's flat country. You can stand on a tuna can and watch your dog run away for two days." He's not far off.

My father's grandparents, the Turners—whom we called A.K. and Grandma Birdie—lived in Coahoma, a tiny town with a population of about 800 located an hour northeast of Midland, in the heart of the Permian Basin—oil country. A.K. was born in 1898 and together with Birdie, they had twelve children, the oldest of which was my grandmother, Dorothy, my father's mother. A.K. was the first person to drill in the Red River, where he worked as a tool pusher on the oil rig, putting him in charge of the drilling department. After that, he worked as a pumper, stopping at each well every day and checking to ensure that everything was running smoothly. He was also in charge of measuring the production of the wells, which meant every day he'd have to stop at each well and measure what had been produced over the previous twenty-four hours. It was difficult, physically demanding work. My father remembers visiting his grandparents when he was young and hearing A.K.'s boots make a sloshing sound when he came home because they were full of sweat from a day of hard work in the oil fields.

For the twelve kids of the Turner family, if you were a man, you were in the oil business and if you were a woman, you were married to someone in the oil business. It was a way of life in the small towns. The oil jobs were paying better than anything else and were hard to come by, so you quickly became a loyal employee of the different oil companies.

Back in those days, it was said that in West Texas, you needed a fifth of whiskey and the willingness to take a drink at any time to get your business done. A.K. had both. He died in 1966 at the relatively young age of sixty-eight. He worked himself to death in those oil fields.

Of my great-grandparents' twelve children, only two—Alec and Denny—were entrepreneurs; the rest followed in A.K.'s footsteps, working for someone else as pumpers in the oil fields. Alec and Denny, however, had bigger ambitions. Rather than being content to work for someone else and grind out a living like their father before them, they wanted to be in charge of their own drilling operation. Together they founded Turner Drilling and in the 1950s, began drilling wells in Snyder, Texas, a town of about eleven thousand roughly forty miles northeast of Coahoma, where they'd grown up. My father remembers that his great uncles were constantly going to Oklahoma—a journey of at least two hundred miles—to meet with a bank to borrow money to drill more wells.

Growing up in an area like Coahoma doesn't afford a lot of opportunity for meeting people outside the business. So many people—like myself—were born into it. And so it was that my grandmother, Dorothy married my grandfather, Albert Bynum—known either as A.B. or "Pud" Young. Pud was one of eight children; he had five brothers and two sisters, and like almost everyone else growing up in the area, he too started working in the oil fields at a young age. From age sixteen right up through age seventy-eight, when he'd finally decided he'd had enough and it was time to retire, Pud worked in the fields, day in and day out.

Grandad was a good friend of Columbus Marion, or "Dad" Joiner, a former lawyer and member of the Tennessee House of Representatives and the man responsible for discovering the East Texas Oil Field in 1930 when he was seventy years old. At that time, the East Texas Oil Field was the largest petroleum deposit yet found. Dad Joiner put Grandad to work drilling multiple wells for him. Eventually, Grandad earned a reputation as a "fixer" who could diagnose and solve almost any problem with an oil well. He could listen to a well and know what was wrong with it, almost without having to look. He was especially good at solving salt water problems and companies from all over the state sought his expertise. Even after he retired, he would receive calls from oil companies asking him to come out and take a look at their troubled wells.

Grandad spent so much of his life around oil wells doing physically demanding and exhausting work, that he developed tricks for getting as much rest as he could. Often, when he'd work the graveyard shift, he'd devise a system to make himself as comfortable as possible during the cold nights alone out in the oil fields. An oil tank is hot; it gives off plenty of heat, even if the surrounding area is cold. So Grandad would sleep on top of the tank during his shift, keeping warm in the ambient heat. If he was worried about sleeping through something important, he'd take off his boots and sleep with his feet dangling into the tank. When the tank pulled in enough oil, the level would rise and the warm oil would gradually reach the level of his feet, waking him up—nature's alarm clock!

When my father was growing up, Grandad worked in a field with sixty-eight wells. The family lived close by and the sound of the wells became a constant backdrop to their life. A droning, screechy noise, the sound seeped into everything, a constant companion to daily life. Occasionally, one of my father's cousins would come to visit and spend the night. Inevitably, the visitor would be falling asleep in his breakfast the next morning because the constant sound of the wells had kept him awake all night. In contrast, if my father ever went to visit family or friends who didn't live near wells, he'd have trouble sleeping; he'd gotten so used to the noise that the silence was unnerving.

Grandad got so familiar with the sound the wells used to make that my father remembers my grandfather being sound asleep in bed and suddenly bolting upright.

"What's the matter?" my grandmother would ask him.

"One of the wells is down," he'd say, listening to the sound of a malfunctioning well that only he could pick out of the general cacophony.

Grandad and his five brothers—Rock, Red, Pot, Cotton, and Dallas—worked all over the state of Texas during the oil boom of the 1930s and 1940s, primarily running operations for Goldston Oil. There were so many Young brothers in the business that it was hard to get away from them. Grandad used to tell a story about a trucker who left Houston carrying a load of pipe. He was told to leave part of his load in several small towns along the way. After the fourth delivery to someone with the last name "Young," the trucker asked, "How many more are there?" He still had two left.

All of the Young brothers raised their families in company houses, in communities made possible by oil. My father, Butch, Pud's middle child, grew up in a company house in Kilgore, a city of about thirteen thousand in the northeastern corner of the state of Texas. In that area, thanks to Dad Joiner's discovery of the East Texas Oil Field, wells were plentiful. So plentiful, in fact, that my father remembers being able to jump from one rig to the next without ever touching the ground. One time he misjudged his landing and fell into a tank battery. He got so covered in oil that my grandmother had to wash his hair with GOJO, a citrus-based product made specifically to break down oil and grease. But because Grandma didn't want the oil from Dad's hair clogging up her shower drain, she washed his hair in the toilet bowl. To this day, he shudders when he relates that story.

Dad was often responsible for cleaning the tanks that would get gunked up. A typical well holds 220 barrels of oil and an oil tanker will take 180 barrels with a full load. So if a well is running slowly— doing only ten barrels a day, for example—it will take twenty days for the well to fill. When the tanker takes away the load, there is oil remaining, often the older oil from the bottom of the well. If it sits for too long, it will harden and solidify and gum up the works. And when that happens, someone has to physically go into the tank to clean it. That was my dad's job. He'd hop in the tanks with no eye protection and no mask, and blast hot salt water at the four feet of built up basic sediment (or BS, though we called it "bullshit") that had accumulated in the tank. It was a dirty, smelly, uncomfortable job.

That was the kind of work Dad did before graduating from high school in 1961 and joining the air force. He spent some time in Puerto Rico in 1967 and was stationed at Ramey Air Force Base in Aguadilla, part of the 53rd Weather Recon Squadron responsible for hurricane hunting, before being stationed at Bergstrom Air Force Base, just southeast of downtown Austin. My father had ambitions beyond oil. Not only had he seen the hard work that went into working the fields, but he'd witnessed firsthand the toll that kind of work had taken on both his grandfather and his father, and he was also wary of the potential prospects for the future. He remembers being at a doctor's office in the early 1960s and hearing people talk about how the oil industry was full of dead-end jobs. The industry was dead, they'd said. There was nowhere to go but down. Many people figured after the boom years that had peaked in the 1940s, there wasn't much oil left and many people would soon be out of jobs. Dad had spent enough of his youth cleaning out oil tanks with hot salt water that he wanted something different for himself—and especially for his children.

He also saw the hardship others faced in the community. While oil has made many people rich, it is also risky and far from a sure thing.

It has been said that some of the Turners died from cirrhosis of the liver, because you drink whiskey if you are happy and you drink whiskey if you are sad, and the oil business can bring you both (sometimes in the same year unfortunately).

Back during the 1960s, farmers owned the land on which people drilled for oil. The farmers owned both the land and the royalty—that is the minerals, or oil, that may be found on the land. Today, farmers will frequently sell mineral rights to someone else, but back when my father was working the fields, the farmers would set up toll booths for the oil drillers to pass through on their way to the fields. If wells were being drilled, farming couldn't go on. So the idea was that while the farmers were waiting to see if oil would be found on their land and they could collect the royalty payments, they'd make some money by allowing others to drill. There was never a guarantee that land would produce oil and pay out and, in the meantime, the farmers had to feed their families. It wasn't an easy life for anyone at the time, and my father knew how much backbreaking work was required, with no guarantee of success. Though he wanted to do something else, eventually my father ended up taking the path of least resistance and working as a pumper in the fields. After his stint in the air force, he went to work for my grandfather.

On the other side of the family—my mother's side—my grand-father was the rare male in the area who wasn't involved in the oil business. Pop was an entrepreneur. He had a True Value hardware store in Sulphur Springs and became the first person to mass produce wooden shutters for homes. He built a plant to make the shutters in Sulphur Springs and ultimately had twenty stores all across the southeastern United States where the shutters were sold. Pop eventually found himself in the unique position of selling and repurchasing his own business, when the person to whom he'd initially sold it started to lose money and wanted to get out from under it. Pop bought the company back from him and turned it around, making it successful once again. After some time, he sold it for the second time and made a nice profit. When that buyer decided to sell because he no longer wanted to live in Sulphur Springs, Pop almost bought the business a third time. As they were doing their due diligence, my mother—who often worked with her father—asked the buyer what bills remained to be paid.

"None," he told them. "They're all paid."

They were all set to go ahead with the purchase of the company when vendors started to call asking for their money. My mother, while searching through a secretary's desk, found checks that had been made out to vendors but never sent. She'd find checks for between $50,000 and $100,000 a day. When that happened, they began to wonder what else hadn't been taken care of. So instead of getting involved in a business with debt and creditors, Pop walked away, making the smart business decision.

Pop was the definition of frugal, never wasting a penny or spending what could be saved. When one of his shutter plants in Winnsboro was torn down, he used the bricks to build his house in Sulphur Springs. He read *The Wall Street Journal*—not terribly common for that time and place—and put a lot of his money in gold coins. Pop made a good living and did well for himself and his family, but you'd never know he had money. He lived well, but simply—his two vices being that he liked to drink Wild Turkey, and gamble occasionally in Las Vegas (although never to the point of putting his family at risk).

Because my father worked six days a week, I spent a lot of time with both of my grandfathers growing up, especially after college. And though my father wanted something different for me, the oil business was in my blood. I learned how to drive in an oil field. Grandad had a three-speed gear shift on the column of his truck and he would let me drive when I was very young. I loved driving so I would frequently go with him to check the wells. His job was to measure the production of each well every twenty-four hours and sometimes, after he was done checking the wells, he would take a nap and let me take the truck down the oil field roads where I would either go hunting or fishing; I'd come by to pick him up later.

Family was important to us and we made an effort to spend time together, even though many of us lived long distances away from one another. Occasionally on holidays, we'd drive the 363 miles from Sulphur Springs to Coahoma to visit the Turner family. It was a long drive; it took us nearly twelve hours on a two-lane road with lots of cities along the way. It was rare for the family in Coahoma to make the return visit because the roads were treacherous and oil hands rarely got a day off. It was a twenty-four-hour, 365-day-a-year job. If the Youngs were coming to town, there would be over sixty people for a holiday. Everyone on my grandmother Dorothy's side of the family lived close to Big Spring in the Permian Basin, only ten miles or so from Coahoma, so the line for food for family meals seemed to stretch on for days. We'd all line up to fill our plates buffet-style, but we knew we'd better make sure to get what we wanted the first time around, as it wasn't likely we'd get another chance. We were told, "Don't expect seconds."

Eventually, after college, I spent five years as a stockbroker. This pleased my father because he had spent his life observing—and living—the ups and downs of the oil business and he wanted something better for me. He had seen the toll the job can take on someone both mentally and physically—his grandfather and several of his great uncles died from alcohol-related issues owing to the culture of the job and the nature of the business—and he did not want that for his son. For a while, it looked like I was going to avoid the business altogether and make my way in a different field, but after five years, I was burned out with the stock market and I decided that I either wanted to be in real estate or oil. Perhaps it really was in my blood. Despite my father's misgivings, my mother knew someone in the business and when I interviewed with his company in 1990, I got the job. Just like that, I was back in the business.

Four years later, at the company Christmas party in 1994, one of my colleague's husbands approached me. He told me that if I was interested in starting my own company, he would sell me pieces of oil and gas wells. Here I was, being offered what I saw as the best of both worlds; I would get to be an entrepreneur, which is something I had been interested in, and I would get to stay in a business with which I was familiar and comfortable. I took his offer and in 1995, at the age of thirty-two, I started my first company, Anderson-Drake, Inc.

My family has been in the oil business for over one hundred years.

In some capacity, my family has been in the oil business for over one hundred years, since 1915. Whether it was doing physical jobs like working as drillers, tool pushers working on rigs, or pumpers, or as vice president of operations, or entrepreneurs in the industry, oil has been in our bones for over a century. While it isn't what my father initially wanted for me, I have managed to create a successful business for myself and my investors. I founded King Operating Corporation in 1996 and have surrounded myself with a leadership team that has over one hundred years of combined experience in the industry. From my father, I learned integrity and the value of hard work. I have never shied away from putting in the hours to get the job done and, as a result, I understand the risks and work hard to get the rewards. Having spent years observing how people invest in oil and gas projects—and how many of those projects fail—I believe that I can now say that I've developed what I think is a better way.

Now that you know a little bit more about me, I hope that you'll allow me to show you what I think is a better way. I have seen too many people lose money investing in oil and gas and I think it's time for a change. My family has worked hard for generations and it is on the back of that work ethic that I want to work hard for you. Let's explore what I believe is a better way to invest in oil and gas together.

Oklahoma oil well blowout

A.K. Turner and his drilling crew, utilizing a "Horse Drawn" pulling unit in West Texas

A.K. Turner's drilling rig in the Cimmaron River, Oklahoma.
Mr. Turner was part of the first crew to drill a well "offshore"

A.K. Turner's wooden derrick
in Pennsylvania

A.K. Turner and his wife standing by the draw works on a wooden drilling
rig in West Texas. A.K. is Mr. Young's great grandfather.

CHAPTER 2
THE TRADITIONAL WAY

It's hard to make money the old way,
but people continue to do it.

—Unknown

I grew up around oil and gas. In all my time in the business—even when I was a child, merely observing my father and grandfather working in the oil fields—I have seen how people invest in oil and gas projects. During that time—over one hundred years for my family—it seems that little has changed. For generations, people have invested in oil and gas with money and prayers, tossing their hard-earned money at a deal and their prayers up to heaven, hoping to reap the rewards. While the traditional way of investing has the potential to pay off big and garner a huge return on investment (ROI), a lot of the time that's not what happens. And yet, people still do things the same way, hoping for the best. But year in and year out, investments fail, people lose money, and operations shut down, all because investors keep putting their faith in a traditional way of doing things whose time has passed. As you'll read in the next chapter, there is a better way. But before we get into the nuts and bolts of how to invest in oil and gas with the best chance of success, we have to understand what I see as the deep flaws in the traditional way of doing things. A cynic could argue that the bottom line is that promoters are concerned with paying themselves first, while the investors are the last people who get paid. It's a "taking care of number one" mentality, and it's doing a number on investors. And yet, investors are not hard to find. The lure of oil still has a pull on a lot of people. People are still drawn to the legend and romance and "get rich quick" promises of the oil industry, and so they keep handing over their money with little more than a prayer to guide it. To understand why that happens—and why it's been happening for so long—let's explore the way things have traditionally worked and why people have mostly continued to invest in such an antiquated system.

In my experience, as typically structured, more oil and gas deals lose money than make money. Despite all of the warnings that oil and gas investing is speculative and dry holes are common, investors tend to overlook the risks and just see the potential payoff. I can't think of many other industries in which such a high failure rate would be acceptable. Baseball, which has been around even longer than my family has been in oil and gas, is a notoriously difficult sport for hitters. An average of .300 (or three hits for every ten plate appearances) is considered great. Even in the present day with stronger athletes who have access to year-round training and the latest in athletic conditioning, the league-wide batting average for 2017 was only .255.[1] Carl Yastrzemski of the Boston Red Sox won the 1968 batting title with an average of only .301,[2] meaning he failed to get a hit nearly 60 percent of the time. And yet even by this relatively forgiving measure of success, a baseball player with a batting average of .100 would never last in the major leagues. Baseball teams invest a great deal of time and money in scouting, developing, and coaching players, and a player with a .100 average wouldn't be a good bet for a long-term ROI. No one would invest in a player who failed 90 percent of the time he stepped to the plate. And yet, in oil and gas investing, that's exactly what keeps happening; people keep throwing good money at projects that don't pan out. It's akin to giving a $25 million a year contract to a left fielder who can't hit. Sure sounds like insanity to me.

So why do we do things this way? How did it start and why does it keep happening? Who is in charge and who is paying attention to make sure that investors aren't getting the raw end of the deal? To find the answers to those questions, we have to look back on how oil became the crucial commodity it is and how we got to where we are today. As with most things, if we want to look to the future, it helps to understand the past.

A BRIEF HISTORY OF OIL IN THE UNITED STATES

He might not be a household name these days, but George Henry Bissell, a lawyer and industrialist from Hanover, New Hampshire, is considered by many to be the father of the American oil industry. Back in the 1850s, he was the man who started the age of oil. Prior to

---

1   Baseball Reference, "Major League Baseball Batting Year-by-Year Averages."
2   Baseball Almanac, "Year by Year Leaders for Batting Average."

Bissell's involvement, oil or petroleum was largely considered a waste product (often of salt mining) or was used for medicinal purposes. While the salt mines of Pennsylvania would unearth oil, a use for it had yet to be discovered. Bissell, having observed the primitive means by which this "rock oil" was collected from the woods in northwestern Pennsylvania—largely by wringing out cloth that had been soaked in the stuff—became convinced that it could be used as a means of illumination. With the financial help and expertise of Benjamin Silliman Jr., a professor of chemistry at Yale University, and Bissell's business partner, Edwin Drake, Bissell founded the Pennsylvania Rock Oil Company in the early 1850s, thus ushering in the age of oil in America.[3]

Once Bissell and Drake began drilling for oil, rather than mining for it, they didn't look back. Drilling was a much faster and more efficient process, and it made it easier to collect the oil for use in producing kerosene. The first commercial oil well in the United States was drilled in Titusville, Pennsylvania, in August of 1859. While the well was only sixty-nine feet deep—a fraction of what modern wells are capable of (in 2007, the average depth of a well was 6,064 feet)[4]—Drake's well produced twenty-five barrels of oil in its first day, serving as a proof of concept and slowly but surely encouraging speculators to follow suit and begin drilling for oil.[5]

"INVESTMENT FOLLOWED HOPE"[6]

A short few years after Drake's initial well was drilled, an investment model—the one that is still largely used today—was established. An

---

3   Yergin, *The Prize: The Epic Quest for Oil, Money & Power.*
4   Truong, "How Far Underground Are Oil Deposits?"
5   OilScams.org, "A Historical Overview of Oil Investing."
6   Daily Reckoning, "Investing in Oil: A History."

entire industry was founded on investment in the oil business where a person functioning as a promoter—that is, one who solicits investors in a future operation— would purchase a lease for a piece of land thought to be rich in oil and would then raise funds from

> *A tolerance for risk is necessary to invest in oil.*

investors to drill a well on the leased land. If oil was found, the investors would reap the rewards of their investment. If the well was dry, shallow, or otherwise unproductive, the investment would be lost. At the time, investors were mostly wealthy people with capital to spare. They were sold on the potential for adding to their considerable wealth with their investment in "black gold."[7] Losing money on investments has always been a concern, but because the oil industry was so new and there were so few operations drilling for oil, potential investors were able to take their time and do their due diligence. Today, oil is big business, but with many, many more companies drilling wells by the thousands and promoters attempting to raise funds in the billions of dollars, the chances of success are still slim. A tolerance for risk is necessary to invest in oil. According to Michael Sonnedfeldt, the chairman of TIGER 21, a community of wealth creators and investors, "There will be extraordinary opportunities—if you have the fortitude—in the oil and gas area."[8] Fortitude is the key word. Investing in oil is not for the faint of heart.

Despite the rudimentary nature of the traditional investment model for investing in oil deals, the process has more or less stayed the same since its inception in the early 1860s. Though the epicenter of oil production in the United States has moved from the Northeast

7   VOA, "Petroleum: A Short History of Black Gold."
8   TIGER 21, "The 1% is Cautiously Investing in Energy: TIGER 21 Chairman."

and Pennsylvania to Texas (which is currently home to twenty-seven refineries), oil is not a regional business. North Dakota, California, Alaska, Oklahoma, New Mexico, and Colorado also contain significant oil operations[9] and promoters operate throughout the country, searching for investors to hop on board the next big thing. Television shows like *The Beverly Hillbillies* (1962–1971), a fish-out-of-water sitcom about a poor mountain man who inadvertently discovers an oil well and is quickly paid millions for the right to drill on his land, and *Dallas* (1978–1991), a drama focusing on the Ewing family and their company, Ewing Oil, kept the oil industry very much in the popular culture zeitgeist throughout the twentieth century. Obviously, these shows are fictitious and the situations therein were played for laughs or heightened for drama. But there is some truth to the depictions of oil wealth; there had to be. Otherwise the shows wouldn't have been hits.

Even with popular culture getting into the game, the investment model for oil remained relatively unchanged. Despite the advancements to technology and the manner in which oil is drilled and extracted (the specifics of which will be discussed in greater detail in later chapters), the traditional investment model remains one based largely on speculation, promotion, and hope.

RISK AND REWARD?

The Texas oil boom occurred between 1901–1940 and many people who invested their money in oil deals during that time period did indeed strike it rich. In many places, oil flowed like water (in fact, there have been times when oil was actually cheaper to produce than water), and the excessive wealth garnered by many investors during

---

9   Walton, "The US States That Produce the Most Oil."

that time period drew more and more people to Texas in search of their fortunes. But despite the stories of easy money and overnight millionaires, investment in oil has never been a sure thing. In fact, four days after Edwin Drake's success in Titusville, Pennsylvania, the first dry hole, or unproductive well, was drilled by John Livingston Grandin, twenty miles away.[10] Before technology like soil gas surveys[11] or seismic imaging[12] existed to assist in determining the best sites to drill oil wells, there was a tremendous amount of trial and error involved in the process. Even today, with all the technology, experience, and know-how available to oil companies, "more than one-third of modern exploration wells drilled—costing millions of dollars each—end up as dry holes."[13] Today there is volatility in the market, and with increasing globalization (discussed further in Chapter 5), the riskiness of private investing in the oil industry has only increased.

The volatility and uncertainty of the oil market and the potential for striking untapped oil reserves is actually something that promoters today can use to their advantage. The truth is that most wells can start strong—perhaps producing as much as 1,600 barrels a day. A production on that scale looks great to investors. Extrapolating out, if a well can produce 1,600 barrels a day, even at a very conservative price of around $50 a barrel,[14] you can figure that's $80,000 a day, $560,000 a week, $2,240,000 a month, and $26,880,000 a year. If an investor sees that data and is told that for his or her investment, he or she is looking at a return of almost $27 million on a single well within a year, of course he or she would want to invest! The problem

---

10   Waymarking, "The Grandin Well—Pennsylvania Historical Markers on Way-marking.com."

11   Geoprobe Systems, "Soil Vapor Sampling."

12   Chevron, "Seismic Imaging Technology."

13   American Oil & Gas Historical Society, "First Dry Hole."

14   Business Insider, "Crude Oil Price Today."

is that, while a well might initially produce 1,600 barrels a day, it's very unlikely that it will continue at that capacity of production for very long. You may get a month, maybe two, of 1,600 barrels a day, but then you'll likely see production slow or even stop altogether. Suddenly your investment isn't looking so great. As the oil dries up, so does your potential ROI and your hopes of striking it rich. Instead, you've just watched your millions of dollars dry up.

While this may seem so obviously risky that no one in their right mind would toss their hard-earned money away like that, promoters who sell investors on the old way of doing things can actually use that uncertainty to their advantage. Because no one can say with absolute certainty that a well *won't* produce upwards of 1,600 barrels a day, it's always a possibility that it will. Because it's happened in the past—just enough to make people think it can happen again—hope—like oil, the promoters say—springs eternal. "Remember what happened in Spindletop?" a promoter could say, referring to the initial discovery of oil in Beaumont, Texas in 1901, where a well struck oil and gushed for nine days at a rate of approximately 100,000 barrels a day.[15] This was the discovery that ushered in the Texas oil boom and oil promoters have been making money off it ever since, comparing it to every potential new well and encouraging investors to "look for the next Spindletop." I honestly think it's unfair for promoters to sell investors on what *could* happen (in an extreme long shot), rather than what's likely to happen. It would be like going to a high school basketball game, pointing at a small forward and saying, "He's going to be the next LeBron James." Sure, he *could* be, it's possible, but it's certainly not likely. LeBron James is a once-in-a-lifetime talent, and discoveries like Spindletop are not much more common. But because promoters and investors are both so focused on what's *possible*, not

---

15   Burrough, *The Big Rich: The Rise and Fall of the Greatest Texas Oil Fortunes.*

what is likely, they often don't spend as much time as they should on the reality of drilling and the likelihood of earning a return on the investment. Think about it: if a promoter tells you that your investment can net you an entire year of LeBron James' basketball salary (currently over $33 million[16]), suddenly, you're seeing stars.

Another reason the model for oil investing is problematic is because there's a very strong "looking out for number one" mentality going on. Some promoters raise money—much more money than they need—because they can then pay themselves first from those funds. Currently, the average cost of drilling a shale well for oil is roughly between $5 and $7 million.[17] Yet, promoters will raise double or even triple that from investors. They do this so that first they pay themselves—often a very large percentage of the investment—then they pay the geologists, engineers, and everyone else associated with the well before they pay back the investors. And all of this happens before the well is even drilled. It's still all speculative at this point. In these cases, investors have essentially given their money to someone with not much more to offer than his or her word. And they're trusting someone who is largely motivated by making themselves rich, regardless of whether or not the well is a good producer. Talk about risky.

Recently I was talking to a promoter and I mentioned that I had a $2 million project that I was raising funds for. He looked me up and down and said, "I could charge $7 or $8 million for that." I knew what it was going to cost me to do the project; it was going to cost $1.5 million, so by calling it a $2 million project, I was already figuring in an additional $500,000, about half of which would end up in my pocket—not a bad payday any way you slice it. But for

---

16   Badenhausen, "The NBA's Highest-Paid Players For 2018."
17   Rose & Associates LLP, "The Current Costs for Drilling a Shale Well."

this guy—and for a lot of other promoters—that wouldn't be nearly enough.

"If that was my project, I'd charge double. At least," he said. A number of promoters told me the same thing. Time and time again, I was told that I wasn't charging enough simply because I wasn't building in a large fee for myself, regardless of the results of the project. But that's often how it works, and that's how it has worked for a while. The promoter takes a 20 percent commission, pays his salespeople a 20 percent commission, and pays the engineers and geologists the amounts they've agreed upon, and before you know it, what was a $2 million project has ballooned to $6 or $8 million. And that's before the well is even dug. So if over one-third of commercial wells fail or underproduce, and the promoter pays himself and the salespeople and the engineers and the geologists first, when it comes time to pay back the investor, there may not be a whole lot left.

To return to our baseball analogy, the promoters I'm talking about are like that baseball player hitting .100 who somehow made the team. Major League Baseball contracts are guaranteed,[18] so if that player hits .400 in spring training and the team signs him to a $20 million contract, even if he never gets another hit, or breaks his leg chasing down a fly ball on opening day and is never able to play again, he'll still collect every cent of his contract. It's just throwing money away on a wing and a prayer. Bobby Bonilla, former outfielder for the Mets, hasn't played professional baseball since 2003—but he'll be collecting over $1 million annually until 2035.[19] And the team will have nothing to show for it except a lighter wallet. If the team is the investor, they're going to be left scratching their head. "What happened to the sure thing?" "What happened to the 'next Spindle-

---

18   Greenhouse, "Are Long Baseball Contracts Worth It?"
19   LeDonne, "15 Worst Contrasts in Sports History."

top?'" "Where did all my money go?" The promoter has long since cashed the check and is on to the next deal ... and the next, and the next. Meanwhile, the well is dry. And that's how so many people who invest in oil and gas deals lose money. It's often based on putting their hope and faith in something that, more likely than not, won't work out as expected. And while hope is a great thing to have, unrealistic hope, or hope in the wrong thing, can bankrupt you.

BOOMTOWN OR BUST

Despite the unpredictability of the industry, oil can (and does) have a huge and lasting impact on a town or city. After all, it just takes one lucky drill. Author Bryan Burrough writes in *The Big Rich: The Rise and Fall of the Greatest Texas Oil Fortunes*, "*One well, one fortune. It was the stuff of myth, the El Dorado of Texas Oil.*"[20] Whether it comes from the ground or from the pockets of investors, at least at the beginning, there is a great deal of money to be had and potential fortunes to be made. Oil boomtowns have gone up almost overnight, transforming sleepy backwaters into bustling centers of industry.[21] Not only do people need to pay to drill the wells, but they also need to pay for the equipment to drill the wells, the salaries of the people in charge of drilling the wells, and the methods for transporting oil once it's found (assuming that happens). Whether or not oil is found, people are getting paid.

Additionally, along with oil wells and drilling operations come housing, medical care, commerce, restaurants, entertainment, and jobs. Everyone who comes to an oil town to drill for oil needs somewhere to sleep at night. Their families need to eat. Their kids

---

20   Burrough, *The Big Rich: The Rise and Fall of the Greatest Texas Oil Fortunes.*
21   Haile, *Texas Boomtowns: A History of Blood and Oil.*

need to go to school and their spouses need jobs. Oil influences the economy in several different ways. Houston, Texas, was a small commercial center prior to the Texas oil boom with a population of roughly 44,000. In the decade following World War II and the industrialization of the area—predominantly owing to the oil industry—the population ballooned to nearly 600,000 and catapulted the city into the top twenty most populous in the United States,[22] where it has remained ever since (it is currently number four with a population of over two million[23]). Currently, over five thousand companies in the energy industry are headquartered in Houston.[24]

Over the years, oil has undeniably made a lot of people a great deal of money. So synonymous is Texas with the oil industry that according to a recent piece in *The New Yorker*, "In the popular imagination, a rich Texan is invariably an oil tycoon." And while many have gotten rich on oil fortunes, virtually none of those who have invested have been risk averse or unwilling to lose what they put in. "In places where money comes out of the ground, luck and a willingness to take risks are the main denominators that determine one's future."[25]

"In places where money comes out of the ground, luck and a willingness to take risks are the main denominators that determine one's future."

But there is another side to the boom of the oil industry. Busts happen all too often—more frequently, in fact, than booms. Busts can happen for a variety of reasons but the most common is that the

---

22 Wikipedia, "Demographics of Houston."
23 White, "The Top 10 Largest U.S. Cities by Population."
24 Right, "The Dark Bounty of Texas Oil."
25 Ibid.

wells dry up. Suddenly, where money was coming out of the ground, there is nothing. And where there is no more oil, there is nothing to support the hundreds or thousands of people who have come to rely on it for their daily livelihood.

Boomtowns can become ghost towns virtually overnight. Eagle Ford, Texas, is a prime example of what happens when a boomtown goes bust. In 2014, Eagle Ford was home to 221 active oil rigs; just two years later, there were only forty-five. Workers who used to man oil rigs and made around $80,000 a year are now left fighting for low-paying jobs in the local chicken processing plant. People are hungry and homeless; it's as bad as it gets.[26] Oil is indeed a harsh mistress, there one day and gone the next. Eagle Ford is by no means a unique story.[27] All over the United States, former boomtowns suffer quietly. Pennsylvania, California, Oklahoma, North Dakota, and, yes, Texas are all home to former boomtowns that have gone bust.[28] And yet, none of that stops promoters from raising funds from investors and spewing empty promises about "the next Spindletop."

The main problem with the traditional, and in my opinion, antiquated, way of doing things—as I see it—is that there's little to no offering flexibility, no extended development plan (running room for additional drilling), and little to no possible alternative plans or exit strategy. A single well is drilled, with the result either being a hit or miss. If it hits, great—for a while anyway; there is always the possibility (or the probability) that production will be sustainable for an extended period of time. However, if it misses, oh well, you're out your invested funds. These deals are not structured with diversity in mind. No additional locations exist, nor are there alternatives available other than plugging and abandoning the unsuccessful well.

---

26   Moskowitz, "When Oil Boomtowns Go Bust."
27   Murtaugh, "The Oil Ghost Towns of Texas."
28   Baraniuk, "The Ghost Towns That Were Created by the Oil Rush."

Logic dictates that if it takes $2 million for a project, maybe you raise $6 million and do three similar projects. Your odds of success have increased and even if one of the wells isn't a gusher, at least you're getting something for your investment. But for most of these deals, that's not how it works. Most of these deals are single well ventures and, for a single well program, as the saying goes, "You pays your money and you takes your chances."[29]

Investors often participate in oil and gas programs that severely limit their opportunity of achieving a reasonable return on investment. These offerings are often not only potentially dishonest and bad business deals, but the offerings sometimes obstruct or confuse potential investors' ability to separate the wheat from the chaff. How can someone identify a good deal and what's little more than a scam? How can you be sure that your money has a chance to make more money?

TAX BREAKS FOR BIG BREAKS

After learning all of this—the risk of drilling a successful well, the questionable business dealings, the likelihood that you'll make any money—you may be wondering why anyone in their right mind would still invest in oil deals. The answer is a simple one: tax incentives or "tax breaks." Oil remains incredibly popular for those investors seeking current year income tax deductions. In fact, "several major tax benefits are available for oil and gas investors that are found nowhere else in the tax code."[30]

We're not talking about small time tax breaks here. In today's political climate, it is easier than ever to invest in oil and gas. All

---

29   Safire, "On Language; You Pays Yer Money."
30   Cussen, "Oil: A Big Investment with Big Tax Breaks."

intangible drilling costs (IDCs) of drilling, testing, completing, and stimulating a well, from labor to grease to rental of drilling equipment to "miscellaneous costs" are ultimately 100 percent tax deductible. With the passage of the 2018 Tax Cuts & Jobs Act, tangible costs, such as production pipe, pumping units, electric panels, oil and gas separators, and oil tanks, are 100 percent deductible in the year placed in service; previously 50 percent of such costs had to be depreciated over a seven year life. Of particular interest to small producers and investors is what is known as the "depletion allowance." This allowance means that any small producer with a production under 50,000 barrels per day can claim a deduction equal to 15 percent of the gross amount of oil income from taxation, thus effectively reducing this income by the 15 percent so that 85 percent is recognized as taxable income. We'll talk more about this in Chapter 4.

When you consider things from the perspective of tax breaks, you almost can't blame people for participating in such a risky investment. After all, if it works out, you have a chance of making big money—and you won't have to pay taxes on a lot of it. The lure of black gold is still very strong for a lot of people.

While investors are often cautious people, known for their business savvy and financial prowess, those who invest in oil and gas are a different breed. Drawn to risk, willing to take a chance, and comfortable with uncertainty, they're daredevils, thrill seekers, and adventurers. And those are the kind of people who will still take a chance on oil and gas. Of course, the tax benefits help. It has never been more attractive, from a tax perspective, to invest in oil and gas. Both the producer and the investor benefit from the current tax code. That's true even in situations like those we've talked about, where drilling an extremely productive well can be a long shot.

In the next section, I'm going to use a specific example of a typical oil and gas investment deal in order to explain how the investment process has traditionally worked, so you can then understand the advantages of the alternative method of doing oil and gas investment deals that which King Operating is utilizing.

A BAD DEAL

Having been in the business for as long as I have, I know traditional deals inside and out. And while I can talk about them all day, the best way to understand how one of these normal investment deals works is to use an example. We'll go through the transaction piece by piece to best understand how the deal was structured and how a typical deal would function, as well as the areas designed to make investors see dollar signs, when they should be seeing red flags.

Glossy marketing materials are the most common tool used to attract potential investors. They are useful because being able to hand an investor material with attractive pictures, impressive numbers, and dollar signs makes a good first impression and indicates that they're dealing with professionals who know the business inside and out. Everyone wants to believe that their money is in good hands. Well-designed marketing materials can help inspire confidence.

The first thing potential investors want to know is exactly what they are being asked to invest in. That's what the Project Summary is for. It is usually a short, one-sentence description of the project that includes the stated goals, such as drilling a commercially productive well that generates cash flow for investors. It is designed as a broad strokes explanation of the project—an elevator pitch. Below is an example of a Project Summary for a typical oil and gas deal.

PROJECT SUMMARY

The Wonder Well Venture is a one-well investment designed to develop significant oil and gas reserves, deliver consistent cash flow, and take advantage of available tax benefits.

The limitations to this venture are evident in the first sentence: "one-well investment." As we've discussed, if investors are investing in a single well for a single project, they have only one shot to make money. If the well fails or does not produce as well as anticipated (or drops off sharply after initial production), there is no second chance and no backup plan.

The marketing materials also typically include a description of the proposed well site, which goes into greater detail about the well that will be drilled and how it will be done. Notable in the following example description is that Wonder Well #1 is a horizontal, rather than a traditional vertical well (more detail in Chapter 4).

PROSPECT

Wonder Well #1 is a high-quality horizontal oil and gas venture designed to use modern drilling and completion techniques to extract significant amounts of hydrocarbons from the rich sand in the Rich Sand Oil Field.

The only new information in this description is the location of the well and the fact that it will be drilled horizontally. In this case, the well is located in the Rich Sand Oil Field. Terms like "modern drilling and completion techniques" and "significant amounts of hydrocarbons" are so vague as to be essentially meaningless.

The following is a chart detailing the initial financial requirements—total, initial, and completion—for the well, in addition to the number of units, or investment opportunities available.

SIZE OF PROGRAM:	1 WELL
ISSUE DATE:	MARCH 10, 20XX
TOTAL ASSESSMENT:	$5,000,000
INITIAL ASSESSMENT:	$150,00
COMPLETION ASSESSMENT:	$50,000
NUMBER OF UNITS:	25
ASSESSMENT INVESTMENT PER UNIT:	$200,000

According to this chart, the well is assessed at $5 million. The following chart breaks down the projections for total investment return an investor might expect to collect. If you look closely, you'll see that the numbers in each column ("Current Price" and "Potential Price") are identical until you reach the line "Dollars Per BO," where BO stands for barrel of oil.

TOTAL OFFERING: $5,000,000		
WELL NAME	WONDER WELL #1	
COMMODITIES PRICING SCENARIOS	CURRENT PRICE	POTENTIAL PRICE
TOTAL WORKING INTEREST	62.500%	62.500%
NUMBER OF UNITS	25	25
WORKING INTEREST PER UNIT	2.5000%	2.5000%
NET REVENUE INTEREST PER UNIT	1.8750%	1.8750%
INITIAL ASSESSMENT PER UNIT	$150,000	$150,000
COMPLETION ASSESSMENT PER UNIT/WELL	$50,000	$50,000

TOTAL ASSESSMENT PER UNIT	$200,000	$200,000
BARRELS OF OIL PER DAY	200	200
THOUSAND CUBIC FEET OF GAS PER DAY	200	200
DOLLARS PER BO	$40.00	$70.00
DOLLARS PER MCFG	$5.00	$7.00
POTENTIAL MONTHLY INCOME	$5,063	$8,663
POTENTIAL YEARLY INCOME	$60,750	$103,950
POTENTIAL ANNUAL ROI	30.38%	51.98%
ROI WITH TAX BENEFITS	46.73%	79.96%

This is an important thing to notice because the difference between $40 per barrel and the potential price of $70, is $30, which represents an increase of 75 percent. At a projected yield of 200 barrels a day and a 62.500 percent working interest, that represents a potential monthly income of $8,663 and a potential yearly income of $103,950. With a potential annual return on investment (ROI) of nearly 52 percent, in less than two years an investor would make back his or her investment. That sounds great and it looks good on paper, but what we need to ask ourselves is: On what is the company basing the projected increase in the price of oil? Why is the price of a barrel of oil projected to increase by 75 percent? And what happens if it doesn't? Experienced oil and gas companies know that there's no guarantee that oil will reach these projections, either in barrels of oil or in price per barrel. Furthermore, companies know that wells are a depleting asset, meaning that just because this particular well is producing 200 barrels a day now, there is no guarantee that it will do so two, three, or four years from initial production. In reality, there is a good chance that the well's production will begin to taper off, producing less and less oil. Companies know this and include a disclaimer such as the following in the marketing materials.

DISCLAIMER

The investment projections contained herein were created by the Sponsor and are based on numerous specific assumptions and include forward-looking statements. The results are necessarily hypothetical. There is no guarantee the projections will be achieved.

Understanding that the disclaimer might turn someone off who is considering investing in the project, the company follows it up with a breakdown of how much one can make, including with the tax benefits. As so many people get into oil and gas, investing specifically because of the tax benefits, it is wise to highlight them in the marketing materials.

Coupled with the last line of the previous chart, the marketing materials also might include the example below, detailing hard numbers and potential profit using tax benefits. This is designed to grab potential investors, making an investment in oil and gas look especially enticing. Earlier in this chapter, we discussed the tax benefits of an oil and gas investment, and here they are in hard numbers for the potential investor to see.

INVESTMENT PITCH

Oil and gas development programs may be attractive, tax-advantaged investment options for high-net-worth individuals.

The key word there being "tax-advantaged." The marketing materials explain exactly how beneficial these particular tax breaks are.

Approximately eighty percent (80%) or more of the amount invested may be categorized as "Intangible Drilling Costs."

"INTANGIBLE DRILLING COSTS"

"Intangible Drilling Costs" are ordinarily fully deductible in the first eligible year. The remaining portion of your investment should be categorized as "Tangible Costs," or approximately twenty percent (20%) of the investment. Tangible Costs are depreciated over a six-year period on a decreasing scale with twenty percent (20%) the first year. Please check with your tax accountant regarding your specific situation.

This is starting to sound like an incredible opportunity when investors consider that such a large portion of their investment could be fully deductible. If investors need more convincing, the company's marketing book should break it down with an example:

EXAMPLE:

	$250,000	Investment
x	80%	Intagible costs (estimate)
	$200,000	First eligible year deduction—Intangible Drilling Costs (estimate)
+	$10,000	First eligible year depriciation (20% of investment x 20% 1st year depriciation)
	$210,000	Total deduction (estimate)
x	35%	Maximum income tax bracket (excluding possible state income tax)
	$73,500	**ESTIMATED TOTAL FIRST YEAR TAX SAVINGS**
	$250,000	Investment
-	$73,500	Cash savings from first year tax deductions (estimated)
-	$14,000	Cash savings from depreciation over 6 years (estimated)
	$162,500	**ESTIMATED TOTAL FIRST YEAR TAX SAVINGS**

The depletion allowance tax benefit is most likely 15% of gross income; therefore, only 85% of production may be taxable.

Looking at this example, it seems as though an investor could get $250,000 equity in a project for as little as $162,500 (when the first-year Intangible Drilling Costs and first-year depreciation are taken into consideration). That surely has to look attractive to an investor. A savings of $73,500 in the first year after taxes would make anyone stand up and take notice. The problem is that the investor will tend to overlook the substantial risks in favor of the benefits. For any number of reasons described in the previous section about risk—geopolitical issues causing the price of oil to plummet, natural disasters affecting supply, more investment in renewable energy resources, changes to the tax code—this investment could go up in smoke. And because of the depleting asset nature of a single well, there is a virtual guarantee that, at some point, the well will stop being profitable.

The remainder of the marketing materials may also include a geological summary of the prospect location, describing in detail the success of other wells in the same area. While past performance is not necessarily an indicator of future outcomes, heavily featuring the success of other wells in the area is intended to give the potential investor the sense that this new well may also be wildly successful and productive.

CHAPTER TAKEAWAY

If you remember one thing from reading this chapter, let it be this: oil investment deals have traditionally been done the same way since the beginning of the oil age because they make a lot of money for the promoter. Think about it: if you're in charge of raising money and getting people to buy into your drilling program, doesn't it make sense that you'd pay yourself first?

Oil is a risky, risky business. Like I said, in my experience, many of the people who invest in oil and gas lose money. But the business keeps going because promoters are really good at their jobs and they can sell virtually anything to anyone. People love to believe in the promise of the next big thing, so they toss their money at an investment deal on a wing and a prayer. More often than not, they end up with nothing to show for it except a lighter wallet.

To continue to do things the same way is insanity. So we came up with a different way. In the next chapter, we'll discuss how I came to think of investing in oil and gas differently, using lessons I learned from a friend in the real estate business.

CHAPTER 3
A NEW WAY

SEARCHING FOR SOMETHING NEW

In my line of work, I've met a lot of successful people in a variety of businesses. Contrary to what you might think, I don't spend all my time with oil and gas people—I like to branch out, to diversify, to see what other people are up to. A lot of that time is spent talking about business, for sure, but there are also plenty of social opportunities to be had. The great thing about spending time with the kinds of people who have had the foresight and the ingenuity to become successful in their chosen field is that there are similarities among all of us—and we can learn from each other. There are very few of us who are too proud to take advice from other people or to apply what someone has done in their field to our own.

When you spend as much time in a singular industry as I have, you get to know it inside and out. You see the good and the bad, the light and the dark, the booms and the busts. And from the investment side of things, you see how the deals are done. There's an expression that states there are two things you never want to see being made: laws and sausages. I'd add oil investment deals to that list. It can be an ugly business, particularly if you're the one investing. You don't often get to see behind the curtain, so to speak, to understand what money is going where and, more importantly, what the chances are that you'll actually see a return on your investment. You don't know exactly how much of your money is going straight into the pocket of the promoter and how much is being spent on the actual well. And you certainly don't know if everyone is telling you the truth or just making the deal look good and talking up "can't miss" prospects because they are desperate for your investment.

I kept working within this old model, but my heart was in it less and less, and it affected me personally. It got to a point where I'd spent about two years beating my head against the wall and trying to figure out a different way to do things. I wasn't sleeping well, my wife was concerned, and I spent all my time worrying. I kept asking myself, "What can we do?" I was starting to get concerned about the financial realities of the situation, too. Money was going out hand over fist, but very little was coming in. I knew that traditional wisdom dictated that I should sell my clients hard, but I kept losing clients because they had invested with me using the old model, and a lot of them had lost money. I didn't want to go back to the same people and start hammering them for more and more money—especially when I'd given some of them almost nothing to show for it in the past. And even if I had done that, I would have had a hard time getting people to invest because I'd lost faith in the process. It's hard to convince someone of something you don't believe yourself. I couldn't put everything I had into it because I felt deep down that it wasn't working. Couple that with the fact that people have far more options for investing their money than they used to, and I was really in a bind.

A WEALTH OF OPTIONS

Make no mistake about it: if we are to continue being successful and making sure that the United States no longer has to rely on foreign oil deposits and can become self-sufficient when it comes to the energy sector, we need people to continue investing in oil and gas. But if that's the case, we need to offer people smarter investment opportunities. Today, there are no shortage of investments for people with some money to move around—a lot of them with a much better track record than oil and gas. Information technology, for example, has been a high-performing sector over the past few years and looks to continue to do well into the future.[31] Internet stocks also continue to be safe bets with companies like Netflix, Amazon, and Facebook holding steady as extremely strong performers.[32] Gone are the days of the Dotcom bubble and pets.com, the pet food and supplies company—and internet investment cautionary tale—that lost $147 million in its first nine months before folding.[33] Instead, investors are flocking to technology and internet stocks and companies because in an increasingly technological world, they are some of the safest bets.

---

31 Carlson, "The Best Stock Market Sectors in 2018."
32 Vlastelica, "The Best Sector of This Bull Market Is the Greatest Investment Story Ever Told."
33 Goldman, "Ten Big Dot.com Flops."

Even the energy sector—which oil and gas is a part of—can be a good investment. But "energy" is no longer synonymous with oil. Energy now encompasses renewable energies like solar, wind, rain, and geothermal resources.[34] Often referred to collectively as "clean energy," renewable energy investments have increased dramatically in recent years. As concerns over climate change and depleting oil reserves rise, investors are looking for alternative sources of energy investment. Even the historically oil-friendly United Arab Emirates[35] increased its investment in renewable energy by a factor of twenty-nine in 2017.[36]

So with all these other options for investors, how do we get people to continue to put their money and faith in oil and gas? I knew that, quite simply, the old way had to go. People have more choices about what to do with their money these days and frankly, there are more financially attractive options than investing in oil and gas. There are sectors in which they are almost guaranteed to see a return on their investment (and not the drastic loss rate of the oil industry). So why would anyone choose oil?

Oil will never be a risk-free business. There are too many unknowns and too many moving parts. But if we can mitigate the risk even a little bit and put investors—who must still be open to taking risks—on a little bit more solid ground, don't we have a responsibility to do that? If the industry is to continue—and it absolutely has to—the investors need to stick around. We still need the investors, so how do we attract them? This was the question that was on my mind a few years ago when I met up with some friends for a ski weekend at Beaver Creek Resort in Colorado.

---

34   U.S. Department of Energy, "Clean Energy."
35   Embassy of the United Arab Emirates, "The UAE and Global Oil Supply."
36   Europa, "Global Trends in Renewable Energy Investment."

THE BENCHMARK

Let me take a moment here to explain that I was only hoping my trip to Beaver Creek would be a relaxing getaway. I wasn't looking for business advice. But sometimes you find what you need in the most unlikely of places. Turns out that's what happened here, when I found my benchmark on a ski lift in Colorado.

In business, the practice of evaluating some aspect of your business's performance by comparing it to a high-performing standard is called benchmarking. Often the standard is in a different business altogether. The basic idea is to take an aspect of your business and compare it to another business that does that particular thing especially well to see where you can improve. For instance, if you run an amusement park and you are concerned with line management and crowd control, perhaps you'll use the benchmark of the nightclub industry to determine areas in which you can improve (i.e., wristbands for VIP service, staggered entry, etc.). Without really knowing I was doing it, I set out to benchmark oil and gas investment deals against an industry that happens to do investment well. In my case, that turned out to be real estate. A conversation I had with a real estate developer friend of mine on the chairlift in Beaver Creek changed my entire perspective on oil and gas investment.

"TELL ME WHAT YOU'VE DONE."

Beaver Creek, Colorado, is about as far away from the Permian Basin of Texas as you can get; if not geographically, at least topographically. While the area of Texas where King Operating conducts business is so flat and broad you can see for miles, Beaver Creek is located in the midst of Colorado's majestic Rocky Mountains. An upscale ski resort operated by Vail Associates, Beaver Creek has an elevation of 8,080 feet, or just over a mile higher than Midland, Texas.

Occasionally, a bunch of friends and I like to visit places outside of our day-to-day for some fun and relaxation. A few years ago, we decided on Beaver Creek to do some skiing. Skiing, as you can imagine, is not something one gets a lot of opportunity to do in Texas. One afternoon, I found myself sitting on the chairlift with David Moore, a friend from Dallas. David is a young guy—in his early forties. He's open, friendly, and always helpful. I always have a good time with him, whether it's talking business or playing golf. David became very successful in real estate when he founded Knightvest Capital in 2007. He now serves as the principal for Knightvest Capital and Knightvest Management, a property management and investment firm with over $2 billion in assets including sixty communities and 20,000 apartments.[37] In less than ten years, he managed to turn a small property management company into a multibillion-dollar operation that repays its investors and provides high-quality service to its residents. And even though real estate and oil are like apples and oranges, I knew I had something to learn from him.

"David," I said as we rode up the chairlift together, the sun glinting off the snow-covered trees and making the branches appear as if they were covered with glitter. "I know you're doing well."

"Pretty well," he said, the picture of modesty.

"You're making money but your clients are also making money."

"Yeah, everyone is doing well. Everyone is happy."

"You gotta tell me," I said, "how are you doing it? Because I'm out there hustling and either I make money and the clients don't make anything, or there aren't any clients to begin with. But I know

---

37 Europa, "Global Trends in Renewable Energy Investment."

there's a way; I know there's a way for everyone to make money. So what are you doing compared to what I'm doing?"

David took a deep breath, adjusted his sunglasses, and proceeded to tell me how it was that he'd turned a relatively small amount of money into a $2 billion company, one with happy investors.

"The one thing you can't change is location," he told me. He's right, of course; you can change every other part about a building except where it's located. You can even tear it completely to the ground and build something else in its place, but if the old building was next to a sewage treatment plant, the new one will be too. "So what we do," David continued, "is we find an apartment complex that's in a great area. But we find the properties that are rundown, the ones that haven't been taken care of, that are neglected, the ones that need some work."

"Okay," I said, nodding. "Makes sense."

"Then," he went on, "what we do is we'll go under contract with the property and we'll raise some equity from our investors. Then, once we've done that, we'll get a loan for the property."

"Give me an example," I said.

"Okay," David continued, "so let's say we buy a rundown apartment complex in a good part of Dallas for $10 million. Then I'd get a loan for 80 percent. So I got a loan for $8 million, so I still need $2 million to buy the property. Instead of raising the $2 million, I'd raise $4 million. That way I'd have what I needed to purchase the property but I'd have an extra $2 million to put into renovations— updating the kitchens, putting in a pool, painting, etc.—to make this building in a great location a place where people actually want to live so we're able to raise the rents."

"Sounds good so far," I said. "So now you've got a building that's worth more than the $10 million you paid for it."

"Exactly," he told me. "Then what we do is we either sell it at a higher price than what we paid for it, or we refinance at a higher value. Let's say we refinance that building at $12 million. What we do then is give all the clients their money back plus a preferred return of 6–8 percent. And the company still owns the building."

"So if you're an owner," I said, working through the math, "and you get, let's say, 30 percent back after giving all the clients their money back plus the preferred return, then instead of taking a small management fee, you can go in later, improve the property, raise the rents, and refinance again?"

"You got it," he told me.

"So what if you have to sell?" I asked, thinking that there were certainly times when it wouldn't make sense to refinance a building.

"If we have to sell, then after all the improvements we've made, I can sell for a higher price."

"And everybody makes money that way too?" I asked.

"Sure," he said. "If I paid $10 million for a property and sold it for $15 million, then everyone gets their money back plus some. I pay $8 million back to the bank, then I give the clients back the $4 million in their investments, so that's $12 million. There's still $3 million left over after the sale so if I keep 30 percent of that, that's $900,000."

"That's not a bad day at work," I said.

"Not at all," David agreed.

"So how many deals like that do you do?" I asked.

David thought about it for a second and shifted his ski poles in his hand, preparing to raise the bar when the lift reached the top of the mountain. "I've probably done fifty," he said, tightening the pole straps on his wrists.

"You own fifty buildings?" I asked.

"No," he clarified, "I bought fifty, but I've sold twenty-five for a profit. Everyone made their money back, plus some."

And that, I realized, was the key. That was the reason David had so many clients willing to do repeat business with him while I was struggling to get people to take my call. He made money for them. Again and again he returned their investment plus more, and he kept doing it. Over and over people invested their money with David because they knew that he knew how to turn it into more money; he'd earned the trust of his investors, something that is absolutely invaluable in his field. He's gotten so good at it and made so many people so much money that now he doesn't buy $10 million properties; he buys $30 or $40 million ones. It seems obvious, but the key to repeat investors was making sure that they made money.

By that point, we'd reached the end of the chairlift and raised the bar so we could ski off and begin our journey back down the mountain. But for the rest of that trip, I thought about what David had told me. Could I do that? I wondered. Could I establish a stable of repeat investors who would return to invest with me time and time again as long as I made them some money? Oil is a notoriously tricky investment and, unlike real estate, it's a depleting asset. While a building—especially one you put a lot of work into—is going to go up in value, an oil well goes down in value the second you drill. The best day is the first day of the production cycle because everything from that point on is a depleting asset. Even so, I knew there was something to be learned from David and there had to be a way to apply it to oil investments.

HOW DO WE DO THIS?

When I got back to Texas, I couldn't stop thinking about what David had told me. While I knew that banks weren't going to give me an 80 percent loan for an oil well (more on that in the next section), my main takeaway from my conversation with David was that people need to be given a chance to make money. You drill one well, one time, and it comes up dry? That's it. Sorry but you're out of luck—and money. But if you increase the opportunity by increasing the number of wells, now we're onto something.

Logic dictates that drilling more wells means spending more money, but what about if we didn't drill all the wells we could? What about if we bought the acreage, but only drilled about a third of the wells, leaving the remaining two-thirds available for sale?

I started to think about potential drilling locations like a checkerboard; maybe we drill in one section and we leave the sections on either side untouched—but available for purchase.

And that's where it all started to make sense to me. When David was talking about selling the properties he'd purchased and making everyone's money back plus some, I realized that was something I could do with oil wells. It's just like David said; you can't change location. So if I were to buy acreage to drill and we put down a well in the middle that yielded 500,000 barrels—let's say that's $25 million—I could turn to the next person and say, "This well gave us $25 million. There's a well on either side ready to drill." And we can sell that land for much more than we paid for it because we have been able to boost confidence that the land is going to produce. So, if we paid $5 million for the land and drilling that first well, and we got $25 million in oil from it, just to throw a number out there, and we were able to sell the acreage on either side of that well, we make our money back and then some. And *that's* how you get people to reinvest while making money.

RISKY BUSINESS

Benchmarking investment in oil and gas against David's success in real estate was a very valuable exercise. It taught me a great deal of useful things I have come to rely on as I continue to conduct my business. And while the main crux of what David told me—you can't change location; when possible, sell or finance; return people's money plus some—was valid information that would prove very useful in the years to come, there are obviously some hugely important differences between our two industries. If real estate and oil were the same and investing in oil was as easy or as reliably rewarding as investing in real estate, no one would have a problem handing over their money for oil investments and clients would have been lining up outside my door. Instead of begging people to take my call, I would have been turning people away. But things work differently in the oil business and there is one primary reason for that difference: risk.

While it's true that the real estate market has surely had its ups and downs—most notably during the housing bubble that lasted from 2006–2012, in which housing prices peaked and then declined sharply[38]—for the most part, real estate has always been a smart investment.[39] People are never going to evolve beyond needing a place to live and a roof over their heads, and though there have been small forays into alternative living spaces, (tiny houses and co-ops, for example), most people still want a house, condo, or apartment of their own in which to live and raise a family. In fact, the demand for

---

38   Kenton, "Housing Bubble."
39   Carter, "Should You Invest in Rental Real Estate?"

housing is so strong that, in many places, developers can't keep up, causing house prices to soar—which is great for investing. Apartment buildings, for certain, will always be in demand, particularly as the rising cost of single-family homes make them unattainable for many people, especially first-time home buyers. Yes, real estate is a good, solid, reliable place to invest your money. But oil is different. Unlike with housing, there are other options for energy and the global market is competitive and volatile. For these reasons, investment in oil demands fortitude and guts and the willingness to accept a large amount of risk. Anyone who shies away from risk should probably consider another sector.

RISK VS. REWARD

The very nature of the oil business is a risky one, and that risk is attributed to several of the factors discussed below. To that end, only those investors who embrace a certain amount of risk are likely to have the stomach for the oil business. Of course, there is that old adage, "With great risk comes great reward," which is likely what draws this type of investor to the oil business in the first place. Some people are drawn to the kind of risk and excitement—and potential payout—that comes with this kind of investment. They like to play big so they have the chance to win big.

Of course, the investment opportunity doesn't exist that doesn't entail some amount of risk. Some of the safest investments available (CDs, for instance, which are insured), are subject to inflation risk.[40] And while there are many ways to be conservative with one's investments, if you want to go big—to hit the home run, so to speak—taking a risk is necessary. It's like visiting a casino and sitting down for

---

40 Financial Industry Regulatory Authority, "The Reality of Investment Risk."

a hand of blackjack. If you're dealt eighteen and you tell the dealer, "Hit me," there's a good chance you'll go bust. Hitting is risky and the odds are not in your favor, but if you get lucky and the dealer turns over a three, then you've just won big; your risk has paid off. Oil is a lot like that. Sometimes you go bust on your first hand; you lose what you risked and that's the end of the story. Then there are other times when things turn out your way and you find yourself raking it in. But nothing is going to happen if you're not willing to take the risk in the first place.

I'm not trying to scare you. I've been very open about the fact that investing in oil isn't for everyone, and it's certainly not for the fainthearted. But I think it's important to know what you're getting into. It's very important to me that no one be able to claim that I wasn't completely honest and forthcoming. It's much easier to make a well-informed decision if you have all the information laid out in front of you. To that end, I want to talk about some of the things that make investing in oil so risky. The following are a handful of factors that contribute to the riskiness of the venture.

DEPLETING ASSET

As has been mentioned, an oil well is a depleting asset. That means that the second a well is drilled and the first barrel of oil is pumped, absent a steep increase in oil prices, the well begins to depreciate in value. There will generally never be as much oil to be had as there is the moment drilling begins and the value of the well decreases accordingly. It's a lot like buying a new car. There's a common saying that the second you drive off the dealer's lot, the car loses 10 percent of its value and it just keeps depreciating in value from that point on. After about five years, a new car will lose approximately 60 percent of its initial value.[41] This is similar to what happens with an oil well.

> There will never be as much oil to be had as there is the moment drilling begins.

Let's say a given well has 500,000 barrels of oil available to be pumped. As soon as you pump out 10,000 barrels, you're left with 490,000 barrels. And while you may be thrilled with the initial 10,000 barrels (even at a low price of $50 a barrel, that's $500,000), the reality is that as time goes on, it's going to take you longer and longer to make that much money.

For example, if it takes five months to make that first $500,000, (at a production of 2,000 barrels a month), and the well has decreased in production and now only produces 1,500 barrels a month, it's going to take you almost seven months to make your next $500,000. As the well production slows, it will take you longer and longer to make money until eventually, the well isn't producing enough to make it financially beneficial to keep pumping. When the costs associated with labor, equipment, and operations eclipse the money you can make from the oil, the well is no longer valuable to you. At that point, it's like a fifteen-year-old used car with a busted alternator. Yeah, you could probably keep investing money into it and keep it on the road a bit longer, but at this point, it might be best to cut your losses and get something new.

The amount of available oil in a well continues to decrease the more you pump out. Oil is a nonrenewable resource,[42] meaning that however much oil is available to drill, that's it; there's no more. The

---

41 Krome, "Car Depreciation: How Much Value Will a New Car Lose?"
42 U.S. Energy Information Administration, "Nonrenewable Energy Explained."

earth will not produce more oil in the decades and centuries to come. This is different from renewable resources like solar, geothermal, or wind energy,[43] and so at some point, you have to face the reality that the well will run dry or cease being commercially valuable. While some wells can produce for decades (there are wells my grandfather drilled in 1937 in Sulphur Springs that are still producing oil), their actual value continues to decrease sharply. A well needs to produce, at minimum, six barrels of oil a day to remain valuable (a full truckload is 180 barrels and if the trucks come once a month, that breaks down to six barrels a day for a thirty-day month). A truck isn't going to fill up with less than a full load, and if you're not getting your barrels on the truck, you're not making money. The wells my grandfather drilled produce only two or three barrels a day; no one is making money on those wells. So, when a well is no longer commercially valuable, you can either plug it up or hold the lease and retain your rights to the land for some future purpose.

While wells can produce oil for up to fifty years, most of those years will not be big production years. It's in our best interests to drill, prove up a well, and sell it off in two to four years, rather than keep it pumping for ten, twenty, or thirty years, as it continues to depreciate in value. It's tempting to think every new well is the next LeBron James, set to perform at a high level for years, but it's unlikely. A well might produce a thousand barrels a day at first and everyone gets excited, dreaming of riches and wealth, but six months later if the well is only producing 200 barrels a day—or one-fifth of what it started out producing—those dreams tend to fade. And while these days we can be relatively certain how much oil is available in any given well, we can always be surprised. A well may produce much more or much less than predicted, thereby increasing the risk.

---

43   U.S. Energy Information Administration, "Renewable Energy Explained."

PRICE VOLATILITY

Oil prices are also notoriously volatile. There are a number of factors that influence global oil prices (we'll go into greater detail about these in Chapter 5), but there is a reason that oil prices are often used as a harbinger of overall economic health. Everything from an increase in production (leading to a flooded market), to a decrease in demand, to geopolitical concerns can result in fluctuating oil prices.[44] OPEC, or the Organization of Petroleum Exporting Countries, is also a huge influencer of oil prices. In the past, OPEC has attempted to control the price of oil by adjusting production quotas.[45] Because OPEC is not immune to political influence, politics can also play a huge role in the price of oil as well, particularly the relative political instability in the Middle East, an area of vast oil production.[46]

Additionally, not all oil is created equal. While some is easier to extract—much of the oil in the Permian Basin, for example (though no oil is easy to come by, per se)—other oil is either deeper, requiring more drilling, or located in tar sands (as with Canada's Alberta oil sands), and is therefore more difficult and more expensive to extract.[47]

Finally, once the oil is extracted, it must be transported and stored, which can be costly depending on how much oil is diverted to storage. All of these factors—as well as several others that will be discussed in Chapter 5—affect the price of oil. With fluctuating prices subject to geopolitical issues, natural disasters, reserves, and production, transportation, and storage costs, the risk in oil investment increases.

---

44 Econbrowser, "Oil prices as an indicator of global economic conditions."
45 Sharma, "OPEC vs. the U.S.: Who Controls Oil Prices?"
46 Louidis, "What Causes Oil Prices to Fluctuate?"
47 Taylor, "The Alberta Tar Sands."

SAFETY AND ENVIRONMENTAL CONCERNS

Adding to the risk inherent in oil investment is the potential for spills or other accidents that can be dangerous, damaging, or even deadly. Oil spills quickly become notorious. You'd have a difficult time finding someone over the age of thirty who is unfamiliar with the Exxon Valdez oil spill of 1989, in which a tanker carrying crude oil ran aground and 11 million gallons of oil were spilled along the Alaskan coastline;[48] as of 2014, tens of thousands of gallons of oil remained on the beaches of Prince William Sound. Likewise, the 2010 explosion on the Deepwater Horizon drilling rig in the Gulf of Mexico released 4.9 million barrels (or 210 million gallons) of oil into the ocean[49] is considered one of the worst industrial accidents and the largest marine oil spill in history. Understandably, these kinds of accidents garner banner headlines and immense media coverage. And while newer drilling technologies make oil increasingly safer to extract, there will always be grave concern about spills and their environmental impact as well as the negative financial influence such a spill can have on a company's stock price. For instance, during and following the Deepwater Horizon spill, BP, the company that owned the failed drilling rig, saw its stock drop by 55 percent.[50]

Additionally, working in oil and gas extraction can be hazardous, as the industry has a fatality rate seven times higher than the average for all US industries.[51] There is a great deal of large machinery, noise, and exposure to chemicals that can be hazardous if not properly handled and controlled. Because of the inherent risks to those working in the industry, investors may shy away from investing.

---

48 Taylor, "The Exxon Valdez Oil Spill: 25 Years Ago Today."
49 Pallardy, "Deepwater Horizon Oil Spill of 2010."
50 Chamberlain, "A key overview of BP as a company and its Gulf of Mexico accident."
51 OSHA, "Oil and Gas Extraction."

TAKE A CHANCE ON ME?

Owing to all of the reasons stated above (as well as others), oil investment is one of the riskiest ventures available for the investor. Because of this, banks and financial institutions are far less likely to provide loans for drilling equipment, land, or other material necessary for oil extraction than they are for real estate purchases. While David, my friend from the ski lift, had found success raising some money from investors for his real estate developments, a crucial component of his strategy was securing 80 percent financing for his purchases from a bank. This is not uncommon in real estate. In fact, when purchasing a home, most people are advised to put 20 percent down and finance the rest.[52] Those who can afford a smaller down payment will pay a higher rate on the remaining amount that is financed, but they are still often able to secure financing. It doesn't work that way in oil; you've got to have 100 percent of what you need before you begin drilling.

It reminds me of a story from back when I was a young man, just out of college. I had just graduated, was trying to get on my feet, and knew I needed a little bit of cash. So, because I was an adult, I figured I'd go to the bank and get a loan. I assumed that I'd be in and out in no time with a check in hand since my grandfather had been a longtime customer of this particular bank and they knew my family from way back. I figured I needed $1,000 to get started and, because of who I was, I wouldn't have a problem. So, I walked in, sat down with a banker, and told him, "Hello, I'd like a loan for $1,000."

The banker looked at me and blinked. After a minute he asked, "What are you going to use as collateral?"

---

52 *Forbes*, "Buying a House? Here Are 6 Reasons to Love a 20% Down Payment."

I swallowed. I had no idea what he was talking about. "I don't need collateral," I said, "I need $1,000."

"To get a loan," he explained to me, "you need to have collateral."

I was starting to feel like an idiot. "What kind of collateral?" I asked.

"If you want a loan for $1,000," he said patiently, "you're going to need to put up something worth $1,000 as collateral."

"Well hell," I said, "if I had something worth $1,000, I wouldn't need the loan!"

Needless to say, I walked out of the bank without the check I'd been expecting, and minus a little bit of my pride as well.

In the years since, I've obviously learned a great deal more about banking, collateral, and financing. But in the oil business, the principle remains the same. It's impossible to buy something with 20 percent, 30 percent, or even 50 percent down; you need 100 percent. It doesn't matter who you are; no one is going to give you something for nothing.

YOU CAN'T LIVE IN AN OIL WELL

Oil wells are never meant to be permanent. They're not like houses that can grow and change and appreciate in value if the neighborhood improves or if you renovate the house, add a garage, and put in a pool. An oil well is never going to increase in value. So when you want to raise the money to drill one, you need all that money up front. And that's why it's difficult. With the wealth of oil available—especially in west Texas—if you drill, there's a good chance you're going to hit *something*. So why doesn't everyone just sell these deals and make gobs and gobs of money? After all, the oil is there, waiting to be drilled.

There is a misconception that when you drill for oil, eventually it just starts shooting out of the ground in a huge fountain like we're Jed Clampett on *The Beverly Hillbillies*. But that's not how it works. Oil doesn't exist underground in a lake or a pool; it's inside hard rock. You have to go through a lot to get it out. You're not just drilling into the ground and attaching a faucet; it's hard work. And all that hard work costs money, a lot of money. So in order to drill an oil well and be successful, you have to be able to both purchase the acreage and you have to be able to raise the equity to drill the wells. That's expensive. It can cost $10, $20, $30 million just to get that acreage. Not everybody has $25 million to go out and buy some acreage and prove it up and sell it for $200 million with the potential for drilling. And acreage without a well isn't making anyone any money. There is potential, but it is, quite literally, untapped, and there's no money being made. That oil well isn't going to produce indefinitely, so you want it to pay off now, or as soon as you can. And if you don't have the equity, you need to find someone who does; you have to find a partner.

Here's an example: King Operating found someone who owns 6,700 acres—ten sections of land—on which to drill. But he didn't have any more equity. He'd spent everything he had on the acreage and there was nothing left for equity for him to prove it up and get to the next level. So we came along and said, "Hey, you've got the acreage, we've got the money for the initial equity to get it to the next level. Let's get into this together."

Now when I talk about the "next level," I mean something similar to what David meant. We can either sell the well or finance it, and if we finance it, we're going to get money to drill a lot of wells. In order to get that financing, we need to have a third-party engineering report to tell the bank what our asset is worth. Once we do that, we can start drilling. And that—if we have done everything right—is where the money starts rolling in.

Once I put all the pieces together—combining what David had told me with the immutable facts of the oil industry—I was able to come up with a plan for a different kind of investment model. I knew it would take some convincing. The first few people I mentioned it to thought I was crazy. "Why," they asked, "would you fix something that isn't broken?" They simply couldn't understand what was wrong with the old model. I could see their point. After all, the old model had made them a lot of money. But when I took a closer look at it, I realized that it was broken and I thought that it needed to be fixed.

I came to realize that if we did this right—if we gave people the best chance possible to recoup their investment and make more money faster—we could change the way we did business and make it more profitable for everyone. I know that success breeds confidence and trust and I remembered what David had told me. I wanted to change things up and do it in a way that was fair to everyone. We just had to get started.

CHANGE IS GOOD

Of course, change doesn't happen overnight. Especially not in an industry as old as oil and gas. While many people may point to the advances in machinery and oil extraction technology as proof that the industry is not change averse, I know that the oil industry is a study in contrasts when it comes to

I needed to embrace change on the investment side with the same fervor and passion as we do on the technical side.

embracing change. Operators are quick to adopt the newest extraction or completion technology, secure in the knowledge that if there is oil to be had, all of the high-tech machines and gadgets that money can buy will find it and get every last available drop. That side of the industry changes fast. New methods are constantly being invented (horizontal drilling quickly caught on once its capabilities became clear), and everyone likes to boast the latest and greatest tools for extracting oil. But on the other side of the industry—the money—things have stayed more or less the same since oil was first drilled back in the 1850s. That being the case, I knew that if I truly wanted to change the way we do business at King Operating, I needed to embrace change on the investment side with the same fervor and passion as we do on the technical side.

Of course, when it came to making the change in how we did business and how we sought investors, it wasn't so simple. King Operating had been pretty successful for a long time and making a big change to the way we did things was risky. But then there's virtually nothing about the oil business that isn't risky, so why would this be any different? At first, I had a difficult time convincing my colleagues that making this change was in everyone's best interests. I did get pushback at first, but in retrospect, my timing was fortuitous because at the time, we weren't making a great deal of money. We were having trouble getting people to reinvest with us because we hadn't given them much of a reason to, and I knew we needed to shake things up in a major way.

Initially, it seemed like the new kinds of deals would make us less money, but when I broke it down and explained that the new way would give our investors a better chance of not only making back their money, but of making additional money—and they would therefore be willing to invest with us again—it started to make sense.

Once we made the decision to change, we had to determine the best way to do it. Should we finish out our remaining deals—the ones we'd made using the old system of investments—while gradually transitioning to new types of deals? Or should we make the change all at once, ripping off the Band-Aid, so to speak, and switch over to the new system of investment in one fell swoop?

We decided that the best way to make the switch was to do it all at once. That, of course, was also risky, but, embracing the nature of risk, we went with it. We decided to raise money for the new project. That was a huge risk. Looking back, if that had been a bad well, or we'd somehow screwed it up, we would have been dead in the water. Hockey great Wayne Gretzky famously said, "You miss 100 percent of the shots you don't take." And that's the mind-set we had going into this new project. We knew that nothing ventured, nothing gained, and we were hungry for a change.

Since that first project, we've continued to utilize the new method of investments, focusing on what is commonly referred to as ADD or "acquire, develop, and divest." This is almost exactly what David Moore was talking about when he walked me through his methods for real estate acquisition and management. If we buy the acreage, and we develop the wells, but we sell them—or divest—before we even begin pumping oil, we're selling them at their most valuable. Put another way, if we're the car dealer, we're selling new cars to other people who are driving them off the lot and immediately watching them depreciate in value. Since we know that a well is the most valuable before it's even drilled; that's when we try to make our money. I also took into consideration what David told me about location. "Location, location, location" holds true in oil drilling just as it has for retail or real estate. That being the case, acquiring acreage with the best prospects is key. If we acquire enough acreage—or, in our current deal with the owner of 6,700 acres, partner with someone who has it—we can use our equity to develop the wells. In this case, we can drill ten wells on that land and sell them off to pay back our investors and make money. And with ten wells instead of one, everyone stands a better chance of coming out on top.

A well is the most valuable before it's even drilled; that's when we try to make our money.

Since we've been doing things this way, I've found that not only have our investors been happier—and more of them have been willing to repeatedly invest with us—but we also move at a faster pace, keeping things lively and interesting. Our goal now is not to drill a single well and hope that it continues to produce at top volume for twenty, thirty, or forty years—something that is statistically unlikely to happen anyway. Now, we're much more interested in the shorter term. We want to get in, get the acreage, drill the wells, prove it up, and sell it in a matter of two, three, or four years. We want to turn things around quickly; let someone else take the risk and experience the diminishing returns of actually drilling. Our investors are happy as well.

If we can buy acreage, drill a well for that $25 million, prove it up, and sell it for $200 million, a lot of people will make a lot of money. And while it certainly represents a change to the way things have almost always been done, I think—and I believe our investors would agree—that it's a change for the better.

CHAPTER TAKEAWAY

The important thing to remember from this chapter is that the key to drilling for oil and making money isn't really the oil at all; it's the potential for oil. Any marketing materials you read are rife with the word "potential," and that is where the money lies. While there may be some instances where it is financially beneficial it to keep a well and operate it for years, the reality is that in the majority of cases, it is more valuable to acquire acreage, drill wells, and sell them to someone else who wants to drill.

Changing the way we do business has given investors the best chance of recouping their investment plus some. Because of the short-term nature of these deals, money is made quickly and is therefore available for reinvestment much faster. Considering the current friendly tax benefits to oil and gas investment, striking while the iron is hot and having the opportunity to reinvest is a valuable opportunity. Risk can never be completely removed from the equation and factors such as alternative energy options and political maneuvering can always affect the oil and gas industry. But at least with this new method of investment, investors have options. You'll never be risk-free when investing in oil and gas, but there's nothing wrong with giving yourself some backup. Tightrope walkers take risks too, but they also have a safety net.

CHAPTER 4
THE BETTER WAY

A NEW ERA

The bottom line to this whole venture is that if the industry is to survive, people need to continue to invest in oil and gas. It's no longer the only choice so it has to be an attractive one. And while tax benefits are incentive enough for many people (more about that later in the chapter), many other people still need something else. They want to feel as though their investment is in good hands and that the people they have trusted with their money are looking out for their best interests. And if that's going to be the case, change—real, industry-wide change—is necessary.

TECH UPGRADES

In an industry as old as the oil and gas business, change is difficult. There are those who say they're for it, but in reality, they don't do much to help it along. And there are those who are downright hostile toward it. Truthfully, there are also people who acknowledge that change can be beneficial when it comes to the technology used in finding and pumping oil. Those sorts of advancements make it easier for them to make money.

Gone are the days of my grandfather's era when you measured an oil well with what amounted to a giant dipstick. It wasn't rocket science—it was hardly science at all. What used to happen was that you'd have a pipe in the ground and the oil would infiltrate through the well bore at the bottom of the well. Every twenty-four hours someone would have to check it to make sure that when the pumping unit came back up there was oil in it. If it's dry, it'll hit the bottom and be sitting there doing nothing, producing zero oil. No oil being pumped means that no money is being made. My grandfather used to be able to tell whether or not a well was pumping oil just by listening. I remember driving along with him in his pickup truck and he'd say, "Put your window down." I'd do what he asked and he'd sit there for a minute listening. Then he'd say,

"Okay, let's go."

"What are you doing?" I'd ask.

"I'm listening to see how well it's pumping," he'd say.

"I can't hear that," I'd tell him.

He'd just shrug and drive on. He couldn't explain it to me; he just knew it when he heard it. I imagine it's like with cars. People who understand cars can listen to a car running and tell you what's wrong with the engine or the alternator or the compressor. To me, it all just sounds like noise. I don't think it's something that can be taught; you learn by feel. But that's not the way things are done anymore. Now, to determine whether or not a well is producing oil, there are all kinds of highly scientific and technical methods we use.

In order to determine how much oil is available, we need to understand how big the reservoir is. Oil underground behaves the same way as oil in your kitchen. If you mix it with water, eventually, it's going to separate out and rise to the top. So we measure using a 3-D seismic survey. It's similar to an ultrasound a pregnant woman would have in that we use sound waves to look into the earth and send back a picture of what we're likely to find down there. We can also determine the amount of likely oil by taking a core sample—or a big piece of rock—and measuring how much oil is trapped inside. We can use software to combine measurements from a number of wells to give us a pretty accurate reading of what we can expect the well to produce.[53] It's all a very scientific business and a long way from my grandfather listening from the open window of his pickup truck.

So why are people in oil and gas so willing to accept new technology and evolution in the science of oil drilling when they're not willing to change the way business is done? The simple answer is: money. If newer technology and science help us more quickly and accurately determine how much oil can be extracted from a given location, promoters can use that information to make more bad deals. They can wave sheets of numbers around and spout off about seismic surveys and software simulations to get people to invest millions of dollars in the old way of doing things. And the promoters will get paid. But tell them you want to change the fundamental way you do business with potential investors, and they'll slam on the brakes faster than you can blink. They've been making money hand over fist

---

53   Quora, "How do they estimate the amount of oil in an oil well?"

the old way. It never mattered to them if their investors were getting their money back or not; either way, the promoters got paid. And while I don't like to put anyone out of business, I think the old-line promoters could stand to work a little harder for their money. At least with the new way, everyone has a shot.

LET'S GET HORIZONTAL

No one is eager to go back to the days of wildcatters and drilling prospect wells in the hopes of finding oil. The hit and miss method of drilling has rightfully been consigned to the dustbin of history.

> *The hit and miss method of drilling has rightfully been consigned to the dustbin of history.*

But it has never been as easy as Jed Clampett and *The Beverly Hillbillies* made it look. We've found that the best way to be sure that we're getting as much oil as possible and taking full advantage of the wells we're drilling is to use horizontal wells. Before we figured out how to drill horizontally, the Permian Basin was considered the largest and least economically useful oil field in the world. There's oil there—there always has been—but it's not easy to get to. If you drill vertical wells, all you're going to get is rock and a bunch of holes in the earth. You may drill the well, perforate the earth, and you might even frack it—which involves injecting high pressure liquid into the rocks to force open cracks to extract oil or gas—and you'd end up with 50,000 barrels. That might seem good, but if it cost you $2 million to drill that well, at $50 a barrel, you're barely breaking even. It's incredibly difficult, even with all the modern technology we have, to drill a successful vertical well. You need so much more equity and even though the oil was there, it wouldn't come out.

So we do things differently today. Today, we drill horizontal wells. With a horizontal well, you only drill once, instead of the hundreds of times you may have to drill vertical wells. The following graphic depicts the difference in potential production for a typical vertical well compared to a horizontal well.

A TYPICAL PERMIAN BASIN
WOLFCAMP HORIZONTAL MAP

Image independently created by Michael R. Eudy.

The vertical well on the left has a fraction of the wellbores that the horizontal well has. This means that the vertical well is only able to extract a fraction of the oil of a horizontal well. Horizontal wells are more economical because they require less drilling equipment and less overall acreage, plus the drilling sites themselves take up much less space—all of which results in a less expensive drilling operation.

A typical horizontal well is drilled vertically to a depth of 7,000 feet and then turns on the lateral for up to 7,500 feet. You still have to frack it because the oil is still trapped in hard rock, but with the length of the horizontal well and the placement of all the wellbores, you might have five million barrels of oil right there at your fingertips. That's a heck of a lot more economical than getting 50,000 barrels. But the truth of the matter is that even with a horizontal well, we might only get 50,000 barrels if we don't frack it properly. The marble table I have in my office is just as useful to me in terms of producing oil as a well is if we don't frack it. We have to force the oil out. But with a horizontal well, we

> *The vertical well is only able to extract a fraction of the oil of a horizontal well.*

can do that because we have fifty stage fracks. That means that every 200 feet or so along the line of the horizontal well, we can frack and force out what oil is there. And because a horizontal well can run for a mile and a half below the earth, that's a lot of fracking and a lot of oil to be had. Even so, this is a more economical method of oil drilling than a traditional vertical well.

Here's an example: let's say we drill a horizontal well in the Permian Basin on a 7,500-foot lateral and we frack it every 200 feet. 7,500 divided by 200 is 37.5 so we'll say that conservatively, we're going to frack thirty-five times for thirty-five stages. Each stage costs between $75,000 to $100,000 because, until we perforate the pipe and run water down there at high rates of speed and open up the formation, the oil isn't going anywhere. But once you perforate the pipe and force the water down, the oil comes up. So having a horizontal well with thirty-five stages is really like having thirty-five vertical wells. And if each of those produces the same 50,000 barrels that the vertical well produced, that's 1.75 million barrels of oil. So even if each stage costs you $100,000 ($3.5 million for the entire 7,500-foot lateral), if you end up with 1.75 million barrels of oil at a conservative $50 a barrel, you're still making $87.5 million. That's a heck of a lot better than barely breaking even. Of course, there are more costs associated with drilling a well than just fracking in stages. All told, we'll spend about $8 million on a horizontal well. So even if we only get one million barrels from that well and we sell them at $50 a barrel, that's $50 million. We spend $8 million and make $50 million. That's some easy math.

The difference—and the reason why we can be so profitable with this kind of well—is that we put the acreage together first and *then* we put the money together to drill the horizontal well. If we show a public company that we spent $8 million to make $50 million, they'll buy that all day long, especially if you have the running room. And the running room is the difference; that's what was missing in our older deals. It was one and done—if you were lucky.

A BETTER APPROACH

Just as we did in looking at a traditional oil investment deal, one of the best ways to understand a new deal is to go through one step by step. As King Operating has made the switch to this new kind of investment approach over the past few years, we have seen a great deal of success. We've followed the formula taught to me by David Moore, and I think it has worked out well for us and our investors. Following, we'll break down the components of one of these deals.

In broad strokes, the model looks like this:

ACQUIRE
Contiguous acreage in an area of established production
DEVELOP
Drill economic horizontal wells
Use reserves as collateral to obtain a credit source to fund future drilling
Repeat. Repeat. Repeat. Until we drill about 1/3 of locations.
DIVEST
Consider asset sale as opportunities arise as field's value is proven up.
Anticipated holding period of no longer than 3 to 5 years.

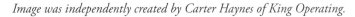

Image was independently created by Carter Haynes of King Operating.

The key to this new model of doing deals is the first part, the acquisition of the land. If we acquire a large amount of contiguous acreage in the Permian Basin, we have a proven location for extracting large amounts of oil. It's not easy to drill in the Permian Basin and *not* hit oil, but there are still some locations that are more productive than others. And even if you find a good location, you have to be willing to put in the work.

Based on the history of the area and measurements conducted in the acreage purchased, the area is of exceptional performance. This all works in our favor because good production means that it will take less time to prove up the location and develop equity. And once we do that, we can sell or divest for a greater profit. For this current location, we initially raised $37 million in capital to acquire the leases on 12,503 acres within an area that has become known as the Strawn Formation.

Because we know with reasonable certainty how much oil is in reserve, we use those reserves as collateral to fund future drilling.

The next step in our process was to drill those horizontal wells we've talked about. As horizontal wells are more economical than vertical wells, there is a greater potential return on investment. After acquiring the acreage in Strawn, we drilled seven horizontal wells. Because we know with a reasonable amount of certainty how much oil is in reserve, we use those reserves as collateral to fund future drilling. What we were able to secure was an additional $49 million to scale up production.

After two years of operation with this particular project, the initial partners in our investment have received more than 130 percent of their original investment back. That is much faster—and more profitable—than a comparable traditional deal. Using the reserves as collateral to fund the future of the project, we have more ability to repay our investors by drilling additional wells funded by the credit facility.

Now the project is at the point of either developing further or hoping for full divestiture within three years with a target price of between $250–$500 million. With the proceeds from the divestment, we will have more initial capital to use to purchase even more acreage.

This new model hinges on the fact that we look at investors as more than the people who provide the money. We look at them as real partners. I like to tell someone who is considering investing in one of our projects, "This isn't just an oil well; we're building a business together, which is developing an oil field." Because once we buy the acreage, we put it in a bucket. Combining our capital and the capital from the investor, we can develop the new project. Everyone is a buyer in this method; everyone's an owner.

I often like to use the metaphor of the shoe store to explain to people how this model is different. If we open one shoe store and the area of town isn't good, or there's constant construction and it becomes hard to access, or it's just not profitable for whatever reason, that's it; we're out of business. But if we open a

> *This new model hinges on the fact that we look at investors as more than the people who provide the money. We look at them as real partners.*

handful of shoe stores and one of them doesn't work out, that's okay; we have alternative stores. There's scalability. If we see that a store in a particular area is doing well, we can expand it, try to attract more customers, or use the revenue as collateral to open another store. But if we only have one store to begin with, that's our one and only shot.

It's much better to have a handful—or more—stores. Then there's an upside if things don't all go according to plan.

Something else I learned from David Moore is that the key to these kinds of deals is completing them fast. We're not looking to hold onto a well for twenty, thirty, or fifty years as it dwindles in production and stops being profitable to operate. On the contrary; we want to divest in three to five years while the wells are still in their most profitable stage. Remember, oil is a depleting asset. There will never be more oil available than on the first day of a well's operation. We want to get in, prove it up, and get out as quickly as possible. The faster we do that, the faster we make our investors money. Of course, there are times when it makes sense for us to hold the lease on the acreage even as we sell the well to someone else. If there's a particularly profitable well, holding the lease to the acreage allows for a revenue stream that is largely passive. We don't have to do hardly anything to make money from that well, and we can use those revenues to purchase other acreage elsewhere and repeat the process all over again. So there are times when we'll divest entirely, but there are other times when we'll want to hold onto the acreage, giving ourselves even more running room for the future.

On an alternative project located in the Wolfcamp A formation, the graphic on the next page depicts the projected timeline for this project using our new model.

As you can see, we project being able to divest in the next twelve months for between $150 and $200 million and turning around within the next two to four years and divesting again for between $400 and $600 million. That's quite a step up. But we have a better chance of doing it with this new approach. We know the general area where the oil is; we just have to go get it. Or better yet, we can drill the wells, prove it up, sell it to someone else, and let them go get it—all for a profit. That's what keeps our investors happy and that's how we keep making money. And as long as this keeps working, time and time again, we will have investors coming back to us of their own volition and reinvesting with us. It's a far cry from the days of investors not wanting to take my calls. Now

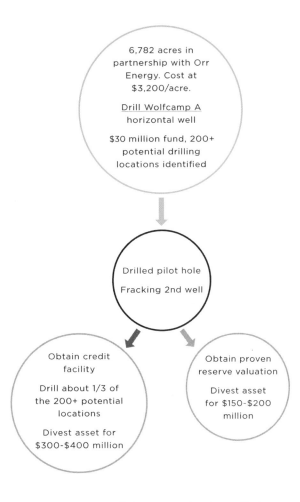

6,782 acres in partnership with Orr Energy. Cost at $3,200/acre.

Drill Wolfcamp A horizontal well

$30 million fund, 200+ potential drilling locations identified

Drilled pilot hole

Fracking 2nd well

Obtain credit facility

Drill about 1/3 of the 200+ potential locations

Divest asset for $300-$400 million

Obtain proven reserve valuation

Divest asset for $150-$200 million

people not only take my calls but most of the time, they've called me before I can even reach out to them. And even better, they've told their friends and other people they know who are looking for investments. Word of mouth is invaluable in the investment business—particularly if you're talking about an industry as traditionally risky as oil and gas. Investors know the tax benefits (more on that shortly), but they may have been rightly warned off investing large amounts of money by others they know who have done so and lost what they put in. "Once bitten, twice shy" certainly holds for the traditional investment model. But with this new model, we've switched things up. Investors are considered true partners—not simply open wallets—and we take that relationship seriously. We want to do everything we can to reward them for their faith in us. So far, we've been doing a pretty great job with it.

The following are actual headlines lifted from the media detailing purchases of acreage in the Permian Basin after divestment: [54, 55, 56]

CONCHO AGREES TO BUY RSP PERMIAN FOR $9.5 BILLION
Combined entity will be largest unconventional shale player in Permian

SM ENERGY TO BUY PERMIAN BASIN ACREAGE FOR $1.6 BILLION

Callon Strengthens Midland Core With $327 Million Acquisition

These are just a few of the headlines about record deals, but this is happening all over the place. As a result, companies will forever want to acquire wells or the leases on acreage where they can drill. So why not let them? We are more than happy to drill about a third of the locations on the acreage we have while proving up the wells around those we've drilled. Then if someone else wants to come in and buy the rest of the acreage from us to drill their own wells, they are more than welcome. In a lot of ways, this new method of investment makes us—and our investors—effectively function as a management company for the acreage. Just like David Moore does with his buildings and real estate holdings, we buy a location (which is the one thing you can't change), improve it, make it desirable, and then

54   McEwan, "Concho agrees to buy RSP in Permian Basin for $9.5 billion."
55   Reuters, "SM Energy to buy Permian Basin acreage for $1.6 billion."
56   Patsy, "Callon Strengthens Midland Core With $327 Million Acquisition."

sell it. In our case, the equivalent to putting on a new coat of paint and resurfacing the pool is to drill a third of the well locations to prove their value, but the end game is the same.

A (NON)TAXING INVESTMENT

Of course, one of the major reasons a lot of people are drawn to investing in oil and gas in the first place is because of the enormous tax benefits attributable to such an investment. Today the tax code is as friendly to oil and gas as it has ever been, as the current administration has doubled down on investing in energy.

It is easier to grasp the true tax benefits of an oil investment if we apply the use of real numbers. So let's say you invest $250,000 in an oil operation. Under the current tax code, you are able to deduct a range of approximately 70 to 85 percent of that investment. The Intangible Drilling Costs (IDCs) are currently deductible in the year incurred. So a range of 70 to 85 percent spent on drilling a well may be claimed as IDCs. Using an 85 percent yield, that's an approximate deduction of $210,000. Assuming your annual income equals a million dollars a year, this deduction of $210,000 reduces your taxable income to $790,000. That's a huge difference. And since you're paying taxes on the lower amount, your after-cash investment is reduced by the income tax savings on the amount of the deduction claimed.

For example, assuming a marginal income tax percentage of forty percent, if you invested $250,000, it's actually costing approximately $165,000 thus lowering your cost basis.

There are a number of ways to take advantage of the tax code for oil investments. Some of the more popular are detailed in the graphic on the next page.

OIL AND GAS TAX BENEFITS

Intangible Drilling Costs - all costs of actually drilling a well - labor, chemicals, fracking

Depletion Allowance for small producers - 15% deduction of all production income

Tangible Drilling Costs – cost of physical items that exist – pipe, pumping unit, battery

Marginal Wells – low producing wells that have been in production 20-30+ years with less than 25 BOE a day

Lease Costs – accounting and administrative expenses, lease operating expenses

1031 Exchange – sale of oil and gas mineral rights (royalty rights) where the proceeds are reinvested in different oil and gas rights – capital gains deferred until sale of new royalty acquisition.

Passive & Active Income - losses can be deducted against business income, capital gains, interest come, salary and other active income sources

Enhanced Recover Credit - over time it becomes harder to extract oil - a 15% credit for expenses relating to enhanced recovery techniques

In addition to tangible and intangible drilling cost deductions, there are also lease cost deductions. Lease costs may be recovered by depletion—deductions (cost depletion) which allow over time to deduct the cost of buying mineral rights and lease rights on acreage on which to drill. Back in Chapter 1, we talked about farmers selling the mineral rights to their land, meaning oil or whatever else could be found there. In today's tax system, lease cost depletion deductions allow for the deduction of the cost of purchasing those mineral rights.

Then there's the depletion allowance (percentage depletion) for small producers, which we touched on briefly in Chapter 2. The percentage depletion deduction equals 15 percent of oil and gas gross income. To be considered a small producer, you must produce less than 50,000 barrels a day. For example, as a small producer, producing 40,000 barrels a day, and a sales price of $60 a barrel, gross production income equals approximately $2.4 million a day. The percentage depletion deduction would equal approximately $360,000 yielding taxable income of $2.04 million. Of the two methods of depletion, each method is calculated on an annual basis, with the amount of the allowable deduction equaling the greater of the two amounts.

Next is what are known as passive and active income deductions. However, a direct investment in oil and gas (working interest ownership) is considered an active income activity. So any losses in this area can be deducted against portfolio income, capital gains, or salary.

There are even tax benefits to low-producing wells. Those wells that have been active for twenty or more years and produce less than fifteen barrels of oil a day are allowed a tax credit of $9 per well, per day. These wells are called "marginal wells." And even though fifteen barrels a day is just barely enough to remain financially profitable, the government wants to protect the operation of these wells by offering this tax break.

In certain circumstances, royalty and working mineral interests of oil and gas can be exchanged under the provisions a 1031 Exchange, thus keeping from being taxed on the capital gains on the exchange of real estate for ownership interests in royalty and working mineral interests. This type of exchange is rather complex and I recommend all oil and gas investors consult with their individual income tax advisor prior to their participation in such exchange.

Finally, the enhanced recovery credit acknowledges that oil is a depleting asset and the longer a well has been in operation, the harder it becomes to extract oil. To encourage this type of effort, there is an "enhanced recovery credit" that allows you to write off 15 percent (adjusted for inflation) of what you would spend on enhanced recovery techniques—that is, anything that helps you to extract more oil.

CHAPTER TAKEAWAY

If you remember one thing from this chapter, let it be this: there is a fair, equitable way of doing business in the oil industry that doesn't rely on paying promoters first. Often, the best way to make money drilling for oil is to divest and let someone else do the rest of the drilling. After several years of operating this way, I can say with confidence that this is the best way to do business that I have found. It is built on a foundation of honesty and it builds trust and openness between investors and operators, critically important things to have, especially in this business.

The oil and gas industry will never be without risk, but at least by doing business in a way that is fair to all involved and not skewed toward paying ourselves first, we can build businesses together and create partnerships for the long haul.

CHAPTER 5
SMALL WORLD, BIG IMPACT

As we've discussed, the oil and gas industry does more than simply provide fuel for cars. In addition to oil, there is also natural gas, which is used for any number of things from heating homes to cooking. And while most of the developed world will have a need for oil and/or natural gas, it is still an incredibly risky investment. There are a number of factors that contribute to this risk including geopolitics, environmental issues, and economics. Each of these factors impacts the industry and can scare off potential risk-averse investors.

However, if we truly understand the environment in which we are looking to invest, and view the industry holistically rather than fragmentally, the entire picture becomes clearer. First, let us look at the supply and demand issues in the industry and explore the ways in which that impacts the risk of investment.

SUPPLY AND DEMAND FOR OIL AND NATURAL GAS

Oil is a worldwide commodity, meaning that virtually everyone needs it. While oil is used primarily as a transportation fuel for cars, trains, planes, and beyond, there are other uses as well. Whatever the use, worldwide, roughly one hundred million barrels of oil are consumed each day. And even though we find ourselves smack in the middle of electric cars and renewable energy sources, worldwide oil consumption is on the rise. See the following chart detailing the increase of roughly four and a half million barrels of oil per day.

GLOBAL PETROLEUM AND OTHER LIQUIDS[57]

SUPPLY & CONSUMPTION	2016	2017	2018	2019
	(million barrels per day)			
Non-OPEC Production	57.63	58.39	60.68	62.95
OPEC Production	39.44	39.54	39.13	38.99
OPEC Crude Oil Portion	32.87	32.68	32.35	32.09
Total World Production	97.07	97.92	99.81	101.94
OECD Commercial Inventory (end-of-year)	2,994	2,844	2,811	2,909
Total OPEC surplus crude oil production capacity	1.15	2.09	1.64	1.33
OECD Consumption	46.81	47.14	47.59	47.97
Non-OECD Consumption	50.16	51.29	52.46	53.69
Total World Consumption	96.97	98.43	100.05	101.66

57   U.S. Energy Information Administration, "Short-Term Energy Outlook."

Unlike oil, natural gas is primarily a domestic commodity, meaning that it is used primarily in North America. Natural gas is used for heating, cooking, and to run appliances like clothes dryers. In addition to residential use, natural gas is also used in the industrial and commercial sectors, as well as the

Oil is a worldwide commodity, meaning that virtually everyone needs it.

transportation sector. In 2016, the United States used 27.49 trillion cubic feet of natural gas, accounting for 29 percent of the total energy consumption of the US.[58]

Once natural gas is extracted, it is more challenging to deliver to the end users than oil. This is largely because while natural gas can be transported via pipeline, it has to remain highly pressurized in order to continue to move along the pipeline. This necessitates that compressor stations are placed at intervals along the pipeline, increasing the need for infrastructure. However, the advent of liquefied natural gas (LNG) is making it easier to transport the product to end users. Now, LNG can be carried on tankers, rather than through a complex pipeline. LNG also takes up considerably less room than the gaseous state and does not need to remain pressurized.[59] Despite this ease of transport, the prices of natural gas are not changing rapidly. Because the market is smaller than the market for oil, it is taking longer to impact the pricing and investment side of the equation. Demand for natural gas is nowhere near that of

Worldwide, roughly one hundred million barrels of oil are consumed each day.

---

58   U.S. Energy Information Administration, "Natural Gas Explained."
59   U.S. Department of Energy, "Liquefied Natural Gas."

oil. However, demand—whether globally or domestically—is far from the only factor influencing the price of oil and gas. As we'll see, geopolitics is a big factor as well.

GEOPOLITICS AND THE EFFECT ON OIL AND GAS INVESTMENT

As shale production in the US has dramatically increased, so has the shift in geopolitical power of the US. In the past, when the US was a consumer nation, the government got more involved in conflicts in the Middle East and other oil-producing regions of the world. In more recent years, however, the US has become a producer nation, rather than a consumer one, thereby lessening the need to monitor and intervene in conflicts in other oil-producing regions. The US, now much less dependent on foreign oil, sets the supply side of the equation, rather than dictating demand.

HOW WE SURVIVED

That shift in geopolitical power rests on the backs of independent oil and gas producers in the US, the vast majority of which are located in the Permian Basin. When Saudi Arabia began flooding the market with oil, global prices plummeted. At that point, American producers and service providers, like drillers, fracking companies, pipe vendors, etc. involved in oil and gas, cut their margins to the bone. The oil and gas industry has long stood on the shoulders of these service providers and during the great downturn of the past two and a half years, many things have been a struggle. Many of the service providers sold their services at or below cost and amortized their equipment, holding onto some of their labor force, which struggled. King Operating was not immune to these troubles. In fact, we continued to drill right through to the bottom and while it was painful, we survived and now we thrive.

Many of the drilling companies that remained in operation through the downturn (and there weren't many) saw their margins hold. But the reality is that holding out and holding on has its advantages. We can make as much money—if not more—at $45 a barrel as we can at $100 a barrel. How is this possible?

When oil was selling for $100 a barrel, there were limited incentives to cut costs. When you're making that much money, you're not paying too much attention to what you're spending it on. But in January of 2016, when oil plummeted to $26 a barrel, we were forced to sharpen our pencils and take a good, hard look at our bottom line and reconsider the economics of the oil well. What might have been a margin of $25 a barrel previously ($100 a barrel, minus $75 a barrel in costs paid to service providers), remained at $25 a barrel when costs stabilized and service providers cut costs. This then became a realized commodity price of $50 a barrel. So while the service companies were on the business end of the great downturn and they had to do a lot of soul searching and price cutting, we all got a lot smarter and leaner.

Make no mistake about it; it was difficult. But we made a promise that we wouldn't lay off anyone due to economics and we kept that promise. This business—and this company in particular—is like a family to me. We may bicker sometimes, but so do close families. Show me the family that doesn't have spats or arguments, but like a family, we always find ourselves on the same side in the end. I have realized throughout my time in this industry that while it might be my name or my face in the public eye, and I am the one asked to speak at industry events, I am no one without my people, and I have some of the best people in the industry.

So, as we have climbed out of the great downturn, we are making more oil than anyone could have imagined. We have applied fracking techniques to oil shales much like George P. Mitchell did to natural gas yielding shales, like the Barnett Shale on the west side of Ft. Worth, Texas.[60] So while you may hear people talking about running out of oil, the Permian Basin just keeps producing. The following chart comes from the Texas Railroad Commission and details the production of the Permian Basin today as compared to ten years ago. It just keeps going up, and up, and up.

> *While you may hear people talking about running out of oil, the Permian Basin just keeps producing.*

TEXAS PERMIAN BASIN OIL PRODUCTION
2008 THROUGH NOVEMBER 2018

[61]

2/1/19

Source: Railroad Commission of Texas Production Data Query System (PDQ)

---

60 Gertner, "How They Lived—George Mitchell."
61 Railroad Commission of Texas Production Data Query System, "Texas Permian Basin Oil Production 2008 through November 2018."

The Permian Basin is 36,000 square miles of oil- and gas-producing properties. The following map shows the extent of the Permian Basin, which extends beyond Texas into New Mexico.

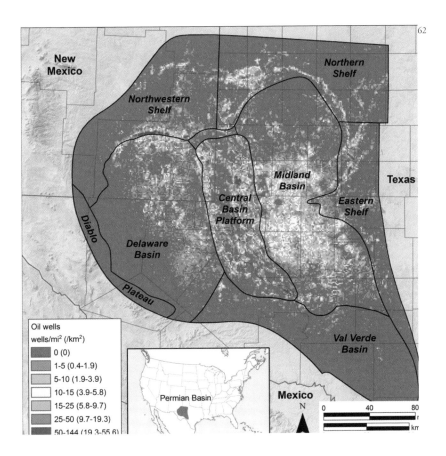

In January of 2017, the Texas Railroad Commission said the following: "The Permian Basin has produced over twenty-nine million barrels of oil and 75 trillion cubic feet of gas, and is estimated by industry experts to contain recoverable oil and natural gas resources exceeding what has been produced over the last 90 years."[63] So while

---

62   Scanlon et al. "Water Issues Related to Transitioning from Conventional to Unconventional Oil Production in the Permian Basin."

63   Railroad Commission of Texas, "Railroad Commission of Texas."

we have weathered a difficult time in the oil and gas industry—a difficult time that surely scared away some potential investors and made things extremely risky for a while—we have come out on the other side stronger, surer of ourselves, and leaner in our operations. As with almost all bad things, we have learned something and we have been able to take those lessons and turn them into something valuable for ourselves, our investors, and the industry.

A STABLE WAY

The traditional way of structuring and financing oil and gas deals included everything from one to one hundred wells, all drilled with equity. Each investor received a "wellbore assignment" of interest, which meant that they owned a fraction of the pipe that went down into the earth and the same fraction of the oil and gas that came out of that pipe—assuming some did. The acreage nearby was the sole prize of the promoter and he or she got the proven undeveloped reserves for free on the investors' backs, meaning that with minimal effort, the promoters were raking it in. Proven undeveloped resources (or PUDs), are defined as "oil and gas reserves that are expected to be recovered from new wells and un-drilled acreage, or from existing wells where a relatively major expenditure is required for completion."[64] In all cases, that "relatively major expenditure" is passed along to the investor.

There were rarely any incentives for the operator to run these wells efficiently as all the money went in up front. Once the well is drilled, the resource starts diminishing. The first check an investor receives is normally the largest; after that, every successive check gets smaller.

---

64   Title 17, Code of Federal Regulations, Modernization of Oil and Gas
      Reporting, Final Rule released January 14, 2009, in the Federal Register.

Instead of drilling on land that's owned by someone else, we want to make sure that the acreage and the wellbore are owned by the same partners. Then, we set it up so that the partners—which is how we like to think of our investors—get their money back first, while the managers only get theirs back after payout. In the old way, there's

> *In the new way of doing things, incentives are aligned between managers and partners.*

generally never any discussion about payout. Promoters never say anything about payout because they've already gotten paid; it doesn't matter to them. Not only does this make the entire operation overall less risky for everyone—though there's always the risk of drilling dry holes—but it gives you a much better chance of making a return on your investment and then turning around and reinvesting with us again, so that we can keep doing it.

This way of doing business also mitigates a great deal of the risk inherent in the geopolitical issues we discussed earlier. Because the Permian Basin is so productive, control has shifted to the United States. Now, we are in control and when we are in control, so are our investors. The stability that control brings to the industry cannot be overstated. In large part, that stability has allowed us to expand and to do the deals we want to do—with the new method of investing—without worrying about

> *Because the Permian Basin is so productive, control has shifted to the United States.*

promoters or outside factors forcing our hand. It's liberating to be in control and we are thrilled to have you along for the ride!

———— CHAPTER TAKEAWAY ————

In the past, investing in oil and gas has undoubtedly been a risky business. But over the past few years, a combination of stabilizing geopolitical factors, the fact that the US has become a global producer of oil rather than a consumer, and the new way of doing business that treats investors as true partners, has made investment in the industry a more stable bet (though of course still risky). It is this combination of factors that has allowed King Operating to survive the great downturn and to thrive in the new era of oil and gas production. We are now stronger than we have ever been, with the production of the Permian Basin at an all-time high.

CHAPTER 6
TEAMWORK

YOU ARE ONLY AS GOOD AS YOUR COLLABORATORS

Part of having a successful business—no matter what kind—is learning to work collaboratively. It has been said time and time again, but there is so much truth to the saying that "no one accomplishes anything alone." Coursework for business classes and strategic management seminars are littered with aphorisms like "Teamwork makes the dream work," "There is no 'I' in team," and "You're only as strong as your weakest member." And while sayings like these may be trite, they are also very, very true.

I learned about teamwork from a number of sources. When I was younger, I was a football player—in west Texas, the land of *Friday Night Lights* and MOJO, it's practically the law that you have to play high school football. So I learned about teamwork in the truest sense of the word. Football is perhaps the ultimate team sport in that the other guys literally have your back. If they don't and you're left out there unprotected, you're liable to get knocked down or knocked out. Football is all about relying on others. You know they have your back and in turn, you have theirs. Everyone watches out for everyone else in the service of a larger goal. There's a reason that twenty-three offensive linemen (whose job it is to protect the quarterback) in the National Football League now make salaries in excess of $10 million per year.[65] Teams have put a premium on protecting the quarterback and are willing to pay for it. There's a lesson here in teamwork. Offensive linemen do not get endorsement deals, television commercials, or Wheaties boxes, but their job is critically important to the team. NFL quarterbacks have notably rewarded their offensive linemen with increasingly extravagant gifts. In 2008, New England Patriots quarterback Tom Brady gave each member of his offensive line an Audi Q7 utility vehicle. Clearly, being a member of a team is important. In that sense, every part of the team—even the roles that aren't flashy—is valuable.

Growing up, many of us play some sort of organized sport, whether it's club soccer, Little League, or PeeWee football. Whatever the sport and whatever the level, we learn these values young and they stick with us. In addition to football in high school, I was also a high jumper, which is a much more solitary pursuit. In truth, I was a much better high jumper than I was a football player, but there was part of me that missed the camaraderie and the teamwork of being in a locker room or out on the field with a bunch of other guys who had a common goal. So when I went to college, I started working out with the football players. In the end, the workouts were so intense

---

65   Cluff, "NFL's Highest-Paid Offensive Linemen."

that I gained too much muscle to be able to jump as high as I had before, but the lessons about teamwork never left me and I have carried them with me throughout my career.

WITH THE TEAM

Years ago, I decided that I wanted to learn how a team worked from the inside out—from the other side, so to speak. I understood how teams functioned as a player. When you're a member of the team, you understand what your role is and how it's your job to have your teammates' backs, but I was curious to learn about how one went about putting together a functional team and getting everyone involved to work together toward a common goal.

At the time, I was fortunate enough to be part of a group that was given the opportunity to purchase an ownership stake in the Texas Rangers baseball team. There was a large group of us, thirty owners or so, and I was really interested in getting to know the people involved, learning about the operations, and, of course, enjoying some baseball.

I loved meeting the people involved. Some of them just wanted to be a part of the organization because they had such a pure love for baseball. For instance, Ray Davis, who is co-owner and co-chairman of the Rangers, lives and dies by baseball. Ray has a net worth of over $1 billion from his years in the energy industry, but baseball is his real passion. He lives about a hundred miles from the Rangers ballpark in Arlington, Texas, but he takes his private jet to as many games as he can. It isn't out of the ordinary to see him there three, four, or five days a week, taking in the game.

In addition to Ray, I had always wanted to get to know Nolan Ryan better. Who wouldn't? One of the greatest baseball pitchers of all time, with seven no-hitters to his name and a playing career lasting almost thirty years, Nolan was also president and CEO of the Rangers. I was fascinated to learn how someone so familiar with being part of a team on the field could translate that into running the team from the front office. Incredibly gifted players are notoriously bad managers. Ted Williams, perhaps the greatest pure hitter of all time, was never able to translate those skills into his ability to manage others and lead a team. But Nolan seemed to have figured out how to do both; I was really curious to learn how.

I also got to be pretty close with Nolan's son Reid, himself a pretty decent ballplayer. Reid is currently the president of the Houston Astros, the team his dad played for during most of the 1980s. It's been interesting to see two generations of baseball men move from the playing field to the front office. In a lot of ways, it reminds me of my own family in the sense that we have a family business, so to speak, and generations have worked in the same industry. It's a little bit different than oil and gas—but probably nearly as risky—but for the Nolan family, baseball is the family business.

Another close friend of mine is Dave Wood, who was on the Rangers' board of directors. He was in the insurance business and did very, very well for himself. Like Ray Davis, Dave loves baseball. He had a suite at the ballpark and he'd go to sixty or seventy games a year, so we spent a lot of time together.

Although I wasn't with the Rangers for very long—only a few years—we went to the World Series in both 2010 and 2011. Being part of a group like that, a group that worked together through all levels of operations to focus on a common goal, was really inspiring. I learned a great deal about how complex organizations are run and how all the moving parts need to be in service of something greater. I learned about motivating people to perform well and encouraging those who might need it. I learned about the nuts and bolts of operating a large organization like the Rangers; what an organizational chart looks like; how a team makes, spends, or loses money; and how it invests in prospects and talent. And when those prospects either pay off or flame out, who is responsible and what happens next? There were a lot of parallels between baseball and oil and I tried to learn everything I could.

EVOLUTION IS GROWTH

Just like I had learned with David Moore and his success in real estate, I was reminded that you don't have to limit your inspiration to those in your same industry. In fact, it is often when we open ourselves up to learning from unexpected sources that we learn the most. One of the most important things I learned is that there is always something else to learn. No matter how long I remain in oil and gas, I will never know everything. And I hope not. I hope that there are still new technologies being invented, new methods for extracting oil being discovered, and new ways of investing and reaping profits.

In the early 2000s, Major League Baseball underwent a statistical renaissance with the advent of Billy Beane's Moneyball. Moneyball focused on the importance of investing in undervalued players and trading them at their maximum value. In this way, players were affordable and performed well at specific tasks. Moneyball became not about getting the best players (and paying high prices for them) but about getting the right ones.

The Moneyball philosophy reminds me a lot of the way we've started to do business at King Operating. We're not paying

If baseball can still evolve, so can the oil and gas industry.

excessive amounts of money for proven performers. Instead, we're investing reasonable amounts in acreage and wells and selling them off when they prove they've got the goods. If baseball can still evolve, so can the oil and gas industry.

EVEN SUCCESSFUL PEOPLE NEED MENTORS

Over the years, I have learned a great deal about the importance of having a strong mentor, someone you can trust to steer you in the right direction. That's not to say that your mentor will keep you from making mistakes; on the contrary, they will let you make your own mistakes because they know that that's how you learn. Throughout my career, I've had a lot of people whom I would consider to be mentors.

There is often a misconception that you only need mentors when you're young and starting out—that once you've made it, you don't need to ask anyone for advice anymore. Nothing could be further from the truth. Everyone needs someone to look to for advice and counsel, even if you're the most powerful person in the room. I have found that it doesn't pay to be too proud in business and to believe that you have all the answers, as that is almost certainly not the case.

There are a number of people whom I consider to be my mentors; some of them know it and some of them don't. Bobby Lyle is someone I look to for advice all the time. At a recent lunch with Bobby, I spent a lot of time bouncing ideas off of him and getting feedback. Bobby is a very important guy in the industry. He's a big player and has been for a long time. The Lyle School of Engineering at Southern Methodist University is named after Bobby. He founded Lyco Energy Corporation in 1981 and spent over twenty-five years leading the charge in oil and gas. Bobby knows the business inside and out and he's always willing to talk, offer suggestions, or ask the hard questions.

I trust Bobby implicitly. A while back when he sold his stake in his company, I met with him for a chat. He told me, "Hey, I've got a couple of guys that work for me that want to consult. They don't want to go full time, but they'll be consultants for you on your upcoming projects. They're two engineers."

"They're hired," I said immediately. If Bobby recommends someone to me, I know they're good at what they do and they can be trusted. That's another thing a mentor provides; his or her word. You get to know someone well enough and you learn that the people they support are the kind of people you want to be in business with. I know Bobby would never recommend anyone to me that he wouldn't work with himself. His recommendation was as close to a guarantee as you can get.

Then there are those mentors who probably don't even know the effect they have had on you. Trevor Rees-Jones is that kind of person for me. Unlike Bobby, I can't just call Trevor up and propose a quick lunch; he's worth over $5 billion so it's not like he has time to sit down and shoot the breeze. But when I have gotten the chance to speak with him, what he's told me has been incredibly helpful.

I was flying on Trevor's plane with him once as he had just donated $25 million to the Boy Scouts of America—an organization that both Bobby Lyle and I are heavily involved in. We started talking about the industry and I asked him, "What are you doing right now?"

"Oh," he said, leaning back in his seat, "well right now we're drilling. I've got four rigs running." He explained that what he had done was taken some land north of Fort Worth near Alliance Airport and drilled. He'd partnered with Ross Perot Jr., who owned all the land in that area and squared off the acreage and drilled a well in each corner. He wanted to show exactly how thick the zone was in all four corners to demonstrate how profitable that acreage could be. Ross Perot Jr. knew that if he had taken that acreage to a public company and offered to sell it, they would have given him $20 million to lease it and drilled their own wells. But instead, Trevor came in and partnered with Ross and said, "Let's prove it up and sell it!" He knew that if he did that and he took it to a public company, the company would give him maximum value for it. If he only drilled one well in all that acreage, they'd argue that without wells drilled on the other side, they couldn't give him anything on the rest of the land. So he took care of that by drilling in each corner. Before he'd done anything beyond drilling the wells, Quicksilver, who was hungry for acreage in the Barnett Shale, bought it for $1.3 billion. After splitting that with Ross Perot Jr., he walked away with something like $400 million after taxes.

At the time, I had zero rigs running myself and I wasn't making any money. This was during the period in my career when I was having a hard time getting people to reinvest with me and I was scrambling to keep things afloat.

"Why?" I asked him. I figured that someone who was already worth over $5 billion didn't need to be getting his hands dirty drilling wells; leave that for someone like me who still needs to make his bones.

"I like making money," he said, very simply, "but I like giving it away even more. If I drill, I can make money and then I can give it away." It's validating to see that people like Trevor, who don't need the equity I need, are doing things the same way that we are.

Trevor is rightly famous for his wealth, but he should be equally famous for his generosity. His foundation, the Rees-Jones Foundation, provides support and funding to programs like the Boy Scouts of America, the Dallas Arboretum, and the Dallas Museum of Nature and Science. That is another thing I learned from Trevor; being wealthy is one thing, but being generous with that wealth is infinitely more satisfying.

In addition to Bobby Lyle and Trevor Rees-Jones, I also spend a lot of time with Waring Partridge, a friend and investor of mine who always gives great advice and is very encouraging. I met Waring as part of TIGER 21 in New York. He lives in Connecticut and is very active at Yale University, where he is on the board of directors at the Gruber Foundation, which honors individuals in a variety of fields.

In a recent conversation, Waring recently told me, "Jay, I love the way you're buying land cheap and developing it. Then you have an exit strategy. It's not just that you're buying the land cheap but you have a plan for how you're going to get out of this whole thing."

He's right; we do have a plan. And it's working for us. Right now, we have acreage in Howard County that we've bought for $3,200 an acre, which is dirt cheap. It's not all together but we have ten sections of land totaling 6,700 acres. That's half the size of Manhattan. We'll have more than that in Colorado leased up for our next deal too— land that we've bought for $1,000 an acre, which we hope to sell for between $5,000 and $10,000 an acre once we develop it.

Waring likes what we're doing. And sometimes it's nice to get that kind of positive feedback from someone who has invested with you. He wouldn't be shy to tell me if he thought we were screwing up, but the fact that he's pleased with what we're doing and the way we're conducting business and our investment deals gives me confidence that we're doing something right. It's feedback like that that helps to push us forward when things get tough. Granted, things have been a lot easier since we switched to this kind of investment system, but it's still nice to know that we're making people happy.

I also rely on David Boyett a great deal. David is a management consultant whom I routinely look to for advice. He's been a huge help to me over the years because David is always reminding me to ask the important questions and to make sure I'm satisfied with the answers.

"Ask questions," he's always saying. "Ask clarifying questions, make sure you understand it, make sure you know what everybody in your company is doing. Make sure they're on the right path, make sure they have an end goal." David is always reminding me that people can have a tendency to be lazy unless you push them. "Push them to do something," he tells me. "That's how you get people's best work."

Of course, mentors come in all shapes and sizes, and they are not necessarily huge successes or even people in the same field or line of work. My father has been a huge influence on me, not only because he supports me, but because he always asks questions and makes me consider the important issues. My father is not a risk taker. He has never invested in oil and gas. It wouldn't make a difference to him if it was $5 or $5 million; he's not going to hand over his hard-earned money. So he never got anywhere close to what I have achieved in the business. Regardless, he's still someone I go to for advice. Perhaps we always feel that way about our fathers; like they're a guiding force in our lives. But I know in my case, my dad will always listen with an open mind and ask the important questions.

My wife is also a big supporter and help to me. More than anyone, she keeps me grounded. She works in the business, too, so she understands it and she's always making sure that I keep the bottom line in sight and that I'm not spending money on things that have little chance of return. Like my father, she is also not a risk taker. But I think it's important to have people like that in my life. My wife is my rock; she's the one whom I come home to at the end of the day and she's what makes it all worth it.

I suspect that for as long as I remain in this business—and likely beyond that—I will never stop collecting mentors. I hope not. I hope I can always find people who inspire me and who can teach me new things. It has been said that the day we stop learning is the day we die and I'd have to agree with that. After all, if I had decided a few years back that I knew everything there was to know about investing in oil and gas, I never would have been open to David Moore's advice and we wouldn't find ourselves in the positive position we're in today. So I have learned that while talking is important, listening is twice as valuable.

A TRUE PARTNERSHIP

Anyone who comes to me and wants to invest—or anyone I approach about investing—is going to get nothing less than 100 percent truth. I will tell them our plan; I will show them a prospect and our marketing materials. I will walk them through it step by step and explain the process from beginning to end. I will give them a complete oral history of the company or the oil industry in the country if they want it. I will do this because of course I want them on board, but I also want them to trust me. I want them to know that I'm a straight shooter and I'm never going to take their money and run. If I did that, I'd certainly never get them to invest with me again and they would never recommend a King Operating investment to their friends. In this business, when we're dealing with large investments, word of mouth is key. And negative word of mouth can sink you faster than a dry well. It's a proven fact that people are far more likely to complain about a bad experience than they are to tell people about a good one. As a result, the good experiences need to be ten times better. So when people have a good experience with King Operating, I want them to share it with others; I want them to shout it from the rooftops! Positive word of mouth is more valuable than any advertising we could do.

Beyond good word of mouth and repeat investors, I am excited about the way we're doing business these days. I want to share it with people. I like telling people about it because it's exciting and it has been so successful for us that I can't help but share. It's like when your kid gets straight As in school or hits a home run in Little League. You're so proud that you want to tell everyone. I'm sure I sound like a proud father when I talk about our successful deals with potential investors. But that's okay. I am proud and I want people to know what we're doing.

Instead of investors simply providing the money and being essentially nameless banks for King Operating's projects, they are true business partners. These days, when I approach someone about investing in one of our projects, I always make sure they understand that if they need me—if they have questions or want more information or updates and want to know how things are going—I am always available to them because we are true partners. There is no employer/employee situation happening. No superior and subordinate. Sure, King Operating are the ones purchasing the acreage and drilling the wells—and we are often partnering with other companies to do so—but we know that we couldn't do any of what we're doing without the investors and as such, our investors have become equal partners. We need to treat them that way. They have a right to know what is happening with their money at any point and what it is being spent on. We're very open and honest about that because we want them to trust us. Transparency is key among business partners. I have learned that over the years and it's something I've taken to heart.

The true nature of a partnership is that you look out for each other—just like teammates on a football field. This means that when we divest, which is the ultimate plan for most of our projects after we've proven them up, we take care of our investors.

Successful partnerships in the business world have become legendary. Some of them have led to the most successful companies of the current century. Everything from the computer on your desk to the ice cream in your freezer can be attributed to a partnership that worked. Apple (Steve Jobs and Steve Wozniak), Microsoft (Bill Gates and Paul Allen), and even Ben & Jerry's (Ben Cohen and Jerry Greenfield) are examples of successful business partnerships that demonstrate what can happen when people work together toward a common goal. That is what we're trying to do here. Our investors and King Operating are two halves of a whole. We work together.

> *"If everyone is moving forward together, then success takes care of itself." – Henry Ford*

Sometimes it's helpful for me to think of it in sports terms; it makes it easier to understand. It's like King Operating is the coach and the investors are the quarterback. In the National Football League, there are great coaches and there are great quarterbacks, but when the two combine, something magical happens. You get a Bill Belichick/ Tom Brady or a Bill Walsh/Joe Montana combination once in a generation. And when it works, it's truly something special to behold.

Why can't we do that with our investors? Why can't we work together—with a smart game plan and the right preparation—and become a great team? Just because that isn't how things have tradi-tionally worked in the past doesn't mean that's not how we should do it going forward. Teams haven't traditionally been in the business of sending sixth-round draft picks onto the field to win playoff games, either, but five Super Bowl titles later, that's worked out pretty well for Belichick and Brady's New England Patriots. Just because no one has done it before doesn't mean we shouldn't give it a try. Who knows? We might create something that others will be emulating years from now, watching our success and trying to figure out how they can replicate it.

> *Our investors and King Operating are two halves of a whole. We work together.*

MORE OPTIONS MEANS MORE CHANCES

Right now, as mentioned earlier, we have a project going on in Howard County. We've spent $3,200 an acre for 6,700 acres, so a little over $21 million. We've drilled our first horizontal well and we have $25 million committed. But what we also have is 200-plus drilling locations that we've identified, which is really exciting.

What does all of this mean to an investor? Well, let's say you have ten sections of land and you can drill eight wells per section; that's eighty wells. You can drill eighty wells in that acreage into that one formation. And you've proven it up so you know it's productive. Now if you found another formation that is also productive, and you prove that up to an investor, that's another eighty locations. Do that a few times and before you know it, you've got a lot of possible wells on your hands! Our goal in this current project is to prove up at least three different locations with productive formations at different depths. With eighty locations to drill in each one, all of a sudden, we're talking about a *lot* of locations—240 to be exact!

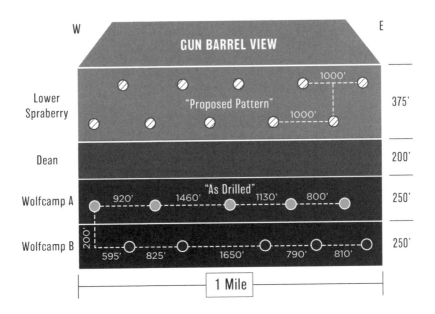

The difference between what we're doing and what a public company would do is that we're essentially setting up a situation for a public company to come in and take advantage of us. They see what we've done—we've taken the acreage and proven it up, maybe drilled some test wells or, like Trevor Rees-Jones did when he partnered with Ross Perot Jr. and sold off the deal to Quicksilver for $1.3 billion, we're drilling in the corners and showing them what's possible. And it looks great to them. We want to prove the locations up for them with initial equity, use a little debt, and flip them. A public company wants to take the reserves to Wall Street and say, "We just bought a deal from Jay Young and King Operating and it has $5 million a month in cash flow. And there are 200 locations we can drill in the future." A billion-dollar potential income is nothing to sneeze at. That's going to look great to most private companies. And we're happy to help them out. In the meantime, we've divested, sold the acreage and the wells, paid back our investors (and then some), and moved on to the next location.

It works for them because once they buy the deal, they can drill ten, twenty, thirty wells this year ... or not. They can wait if they want to. But once we've proven it up for them, they can drill the wells whenever they want. And by that point, we've sold the deal and we've moved on. What they do with the wells is no longer our concern. We're on to the next deal, hopefully with the same investors along with us. Always keeping in mind that oil wells are a depleting asset, we know there is no more valuable time to sell them than the first day they're dug (or, if we can swing it, before a drill bit even goes into the ground). Prove something up and sell the potential, then get out before you actually have to worry about whether or not the well will do what you want it to, and you're golden. Any sort of enhanced recovery techniques that become necessary aren't something we have to concern ourselves with. We're on to the next thing, and the next, and the next.

If we use the baseball analogy again, we're using our money to invest in 240 prospects instead of ten or twenty. That way, there's a much bigger chance that some of them will work out and give us a good return on our investment. And then we can trade them off—or sell them to a private company—for a profit. And we'll share that with our investors. So if we have 200-plus potential wells out there, we can sell that package to a private company for a pretty great deal, without having to put in the sweat equity of doing the actual drilling.

It's like investing in a group of prospects. Sure, some will flame out, some will become middle-of-the-road players, but some, hopefully, will turn into all-stars. And that's where we cash out.

SMALL BALL FOR THE WIN

When he was devising the concepts behind Moneyball, Billy Beane figured out that you don't have to swing for the fences every time. In the end, singles and doubles can do just as much damage as home runs, provided you're hitting them at the right times. That's what we're looking to do with our current investment model. I'm not looking to hit a home run every time I step up to the plate. Every well I drill doesn't have to be a gusher. Instead, I'm just looking to hit singles and doubles, set up the deals for a public company to come in and take advantage, and move on to the next deal. They can stand around taking pitches and waiting for that perfect fastball right down the middle to hit into the stratosphere. Meanwhile, I've cobbled together a single, a walk, and an RBI double, and I've put some runs on the board.

My goal is to do at least one deal a year. At one deal a year, we can make our investors—our partners—happy. What this pace means is that we are in a constant cycle of ADD: acquiring, developing, and divesting. We can do that over and over and over again. In baseball, hitting singles and doubles is called small ball, but it wins a lot of games. You can't hit a grand slam with no one on base, so let's concentrate on the singles and go from there. In the end, it doesn't matter how you cross the plate, it still counts the same on the scoreboard.

GO FAST ... AND FAR

There is a famous African proverb that states "If you want to go fast, go alone. If you want to go far, go together." There is much wisdom in that proverb, and there are thousands upon thousands of situations in both business and personal relationships where that statement holds true. But in our case, and with our current investment model, we can actually go both fast *and* far. Speed is the name of the game because if we can turn over as many projects as possible as quickly as possible—ideally one per year—then we're certainly going fast. And if we acquire, develop, and divest in quick succession over and over and over, no one could argue that we haven't also gone far.

Investors and King Operating will take on these projects and these challenges as a united front, putting in money, time, and effort to get what we want in the end. As long as we operate as true partners and teammates, there's no telling how far we can go.

For our purposes, the important part of that proverb is the word "together." That is how we're going to get this done. We're going to work together as a team; investors and King Operating will take on these projects and these challenges as a united front, putting in money, time, and effort to get what we want in the end. As long as we operate as true partners and teammates, there's no telling how far we can go.

CHAPTER TAKEAWAY

The important thing to remember is that when we do this, we do it as a team. No one is going to be able to take on these projects or conduct these deals all by themselves; it takes a partnership. Whether you're taking on a partner who owns the acreage but doesn't have enough equity to prove up the land, or you're taking on investors to help with the load of developing before divesting, everything is done in collaboration with the rest of the team.

This works because we all take care of each other. In the end, if the partnership succeeds, everyone involved in it succeeds as well. And with King Operating's new way of doing business, we're not looking for short-term partners; we want people who are in this for the long haul. Granted, our projects may be short term in that we want to turn them around in a year, but we want partners who want to do this with us again and again. We want people who trust us and who have seen our proven track record and who want to be a part of our team. Let's build something together.

CHAPTER 7

WHAT DOES THE FUTURE LOOK LIKE?

PREDICTIONS OF DOOM

For years now, maybe even decades, we have been hearing about the death of the oil and gas industry. People have been predicting the industry's demise for any number of reasons ranging from the rise of electric vehicles to investment in alternative sources of energy, and the fact that, as a finite resource, we will eventually run out of oil. It's inevitable, they say, we're in the final days of this once-booming industry. Those who choose to get into oil and gas now are foolish, essentially throwing their money at a dying industry. Some people have taken their crystal balls and looked into the future and seen us all zooming around on hover boards and in flying cars like *The*

Jetsons, and they say there will be no more use for oil. We'll run out but it won't matter because society is adapting to alternative energy and by the time all the oil is gone, we'll be using something else to power our cars and cities anyway. I hear that a lot; that the future is not in oil and gas, it's in solar or wind or geothermal. The end of oil is coming, they predict, and it's going to be here sooner than we think. We're running out so we better find a new way to fuel the things we need and we better do it now.

TECHNOLOGY KEEPS THINGS NEW

There may be some truth to those predictions. After all, oil is finite. Fossil fuels are a nonrenewable resource, and once we take what's there, it doesn't regenerate. But what many people who predict a drying-up of oil don't take into account is that we are always inventing new ways to harvest the oil that's there—to get into the rock and get out what it's hiding. We have been doing this in one form or another, continually evolving, for over one hundred years. It's what we do. The oil industry may be old, but the technology we use to extract oil and gas from the ground (or wherever else we find it) is constantly evolving. Fracking, which is now a popular and nearly ubiquitous process for extracting hard-to-reach oil deposits locked in rock, wasn't in widespread use until the 1990s, more than a hundred years after the age of oil.[66] And horizontal drilling, which we at King Operating use almost exclusively, and which was first put into use in the mid-1980s,[67] is still ignored by many oil companies.[68] In addition, refinery plant design keeps improving with the use of

---

66 Manfrenda, "The Real History of Fracking."
67 North Dakota Oil, "A Brief History of North Dakota Oil Production."
68 Blackmon, "Horizontal Drilling: A Technological Marvel Ignored."

new technology that helps create better models, which leads to better predictions and fewer wasted hours and energy.[69]

In fact, for every well that's drilled, only about 15–20 percent of the oil is recovered. That leaves up to 80 percent of the available oil still underground. That's when things like secondary and tertiary recovery come into play. People keep inventing new ways to get that oil out. Think about it this way: if you bought the well, it's yours and you own it, but if you can't get the oil out of the ground, it's essentially worthless. So it's worth it to you to invest in some technology, whatever that may be, to get the oil out. And like we've already discussed, there are tax benefits available for doing this. The enhanced recovery credit tax allows you to write off 15 percent of what you spend on enhanced recovery techniques, making it worthwhile for you to keep trying.

Furthermore, there are some oil fields and deposits that truly do keep surprising us. The Permian Basin, for example, keeps reinventing itself. We have drilled into it a bunch of different ways using different techniques and we find something new every time. So while people may talk about a five- or ten-year runway of oil—that being we have only five or ten years left—I think it could well be longer if we keep finding new ways of extracting it.

Therefore, while no one will argue that oil will continue to flow for centuries into the future, there is likely more accessible oil available than we think. Just as we have in the past, we'll find a way to get what's there, even if we have to invent a new way to do it.

---

69 Oil & Gas Journal, "Refining Technology Advances Focus on Reliability, Efficiency."

MORE THAN CARS

The question then becomes: "Even if we still have oil, what are we going to use it for?" The assumption being that everyone is switching to electric vehicles anyway so what's the point? But the reality is that oil is used for so much more than fueling cars. In fact, fuel for cars makes up less than half of the oil we use. Last year in the US, for example, 7.3 billion barrels of oil were used. Forty-seven percent of that was used for cars, 20 percent went to heating oil and diesel fuel, and 8 percent was used for jet fuel.[70] That's a lot of oil used for something other than cars. We have yet to figure out a way to fuel our airplanes with something other than jet fuel on the scale needed to support all manner of aircraft (commercial, freight, military, etc.) so at least for the foreseeable future, we're still going to need oil.[71]

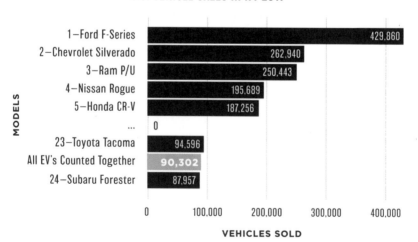

U.S. VEHICLE SALES IN H1 2017

And as for cars and vehicles, while it is true that there is a growing market for electric or hybrid vehicles, they are still vastly

---

70 U.S. Energy Information Administration, "What Are Petroleum Products, and What Is Petroleum Used For?"
71 Klippenstein, "U.S. Vehicles Sales in H1 2017."

outnumbered by standard gasoline-powered vehicles. For example, the American electric vehicle market grew almost 40 percent last year, which certainly seems impressive, but when you consider that if all electric vehicles were grouped together and considered as a single model, they would be the twenty-fourth best-selling vehicle in the US. In the first half of 2017, 90,302 electric vehicles were sold; nearly five times as many Ford F-Series pickups—the most popular vehicle—were sold. And a Ford F-Series most definitely runs on gasoline.

In addition, consumers who buy electric vehicles tend to be both younger and wealthier than buyers of traditional gasoline-powered vehicles.[72] But as electric vehicles account for barely over 1 percent of the overall vehicle market in the United States (1.13 percent to be exact), that still leaves a lot of car buyers going the traditional route. And all of those traditional cars need gasoline.

Beyond the demographics regarding electric cars, there will always be some people who just prefer traditional cars. Electric or hybrid vehicles are not known for their power, speed, or pickup, and those are things that matter to a lot of people. They also tend to be smaller in size and are not a good choice for a work vehicle needed to haul heavy loads. For example, if you own a construction company, it's not going to be very helpful for you to own a fleet of plug-in electric hatchbacks. You need the hauling and towing capacity that comes with something like a Ford F-Series. While electric cars are useful and practical to a certain demographic (city dwellers, for instance), they aren't going to be terribly useful in delivering loads or towing heavy equipment.

At the end of the day, some people just want a big car or truck, regardless of utility. Those people also aren't going away anytime

---

72   DeMorro, "Who Are Electric Car Buyers? Survey Says ..."

soon and as long as they're around, there's going to be a demand for gasoline.

EMERGING MARKETS

Something else to consider when we think about the future of oil and gas is that we're not just talking about the American market. China is a huge emerging market, and while it's a little bit of a conundrum—China has also surpassed the US as the largest purchaser of electric vehicles[73]—it also represents a huge emerging market for oil.

[74]

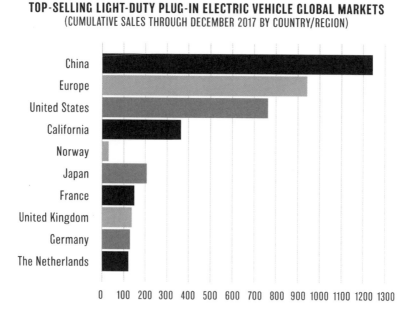

TOP-SELLING LIGHT-DUTY PLUG-IN ELECTRIC VEHICLE GLOBAL MARKETS
(CUMULATIVE SALES THROUGH DECEMBER 2017 BY COUNTRY/REGION)

In fact, China's demand for oil "is growing at more than double last year's pace," at a rate of 550,000 barrels per day.[75] With that

---

73   Cobb, "The World Just Bought Its Two-Millionth Electric Car."
74   Ibid.
75   Rapier, "China's Oil Demand is Growing at More Than Double Last Year's Pace."

sort of increase in demand—and China is just one of the countries increasing its demand for oil—there isn't likely to be a decrease in demand anytime soon.

THE FUTURE OF OIL AND GAS INVESTMENT

As for the investment side of things, I would like to think that other firms will see the light and start structuring their investments the same way we do at King Operating. But in addition to being an optimist, I am also a realist. I know how long it takes people in the industry to embrace change on the nontechnical side of things. There is still a pervasive attitude in the industry that doing things the way they have always been done is the right way to do things. There's a "don't rock the boat" or an "if it ain't broke, don't fix it" attitude that pervades the industry, with people preferring to stick to the methods that got them rich in the first place. Because, make no mistake about it, those opposed to a change in the way oil investment deals are structured are those who have made a lot of money the old way.

If this industry is going to last and continue to thrive despite all the outside threats and competition from renewable energy sources and alternative transportation, we are going to need investors. Investors are getting fed up with how things have traditionally worked. I don't blame them. If I put a dollar in a vending machine ten times and nine of those ten times the machine ate my money without giving me a soda in return, I wouldn't use that machine anymore either. We've got to make sure people are always getting their soda; it has to be fair.

From a selfish standpoint, I want people to look at our projects and say, "Now that seems like the right way to go about things." I want enough people to get involved in our projects that we don't have to worry about initial equity anymore. That would be great. But I think that also goes along with caring about investors. From a caring standpoint, I don't want our investors—or any investors—to invest in a program that isn't going to give them a chance to make any money and that, most often, is going to lose money.

What I want to see is for people to use the new model—or something close to it—so that everyone is giving investors a shot. I just want everyone to be on equal footing and have the same chance.

WHAT DO I WANT?

I wrote this book because I think there is a better way to structure oil and gas deals with outside private investors than the way it has been done in the past. The oil and gas business has been very good to me and my family, but day after day and year after year I see investors losing money and turning sour about investing in oil deals and that left a bad taste in my mouth. Without investors, there are no deals. I feel that it is important to treat every investor with the utmost respect. With regard to all those promoters and people who sell investors on "the next Spindletop", they're only selling a deal, not an opportunity. They don't care if they ever find oil; their wallets are fat regardless. They may not come right out and say, "I don't care about the investor. What's important to me is that I'm making money every month," but make no mistake, that is certainly how many of them operate.

I know people who will take a $2 million deal and mark it up to $7 million. So on a $7 million deal, they're making $5 million. And they know that's a $2 million deal that will never make money, but they don't care because they're getting paid. I want them to either get out of the business altogether or change the way they're doing things.

LOOKING FORWARD

Truth be told, I know there is eventually an end to this business, and I am okay with that. I don't expect my grandchildren and great-grandchildren to be doing the same thing I'm doing, but I wouldn't necessarily want them to be. As generations evolve, so do the jobs we do, and I suspect there is something else in store for them. But the good news is that for those people who are investing in oil and gas now, and who are doing it the right way, there couldn't be a better time to invest. When you combine the cutting-edge technology for extracting hidden oil with the way we're doing business and the global demand for oil, getting in the game now could set you up for many, many years

It's high time they start treating investors fairly and stop lining their own pockets first.

to come. So while my grandchildren probably won't be brokering oil deals, it's entirely possible that the grandchildren of my investors will still be reaping the benefits of the deals I set in motion.

At the end of the day, what I really want is for everyone to get a fair shake and a fair opportunity to make back what they put in, plus some more. I know that if we're going to continue to be successful and if the industry is going to continue to thrive—even with the new pressures of electric vehicles and emerging alternative energy sources—we are going to need our investors. The saying "Once bitten, twice shy" holds true for investors as well. You get burned in the industry, you're not likely to re-invest, and we need those re-investments to continue to craft sustainable and profitable deals in the future. Oil is not like real estate; we can't just slap on another coat of paint and up the price. We have to make sure that we're getting the most value up front the first time. The second a drop of oil comes out of the ground, the value drops. So we need our investors on board from the very beginning, and structuring deals the way we are ensures that we all start on a level playing field with the same goal in mind.

When all is said and done, I want to be able to look back on my time in the industry and say that I did the best I could for the highest number of people. By structuring oil deals the way we are and trying to treat investors fairly, like true business partners instead of simply streams of money, I hope that I am able to say that we are being fair, trustworthy, and open with our investors and we are doing everything we can to make sure everyone gets a fair shake. I hope you'll join me as we do some great work together.

CONCLUSION

I hope that by now you understand that the way we try to structure our projects at King Operating is different, and we believe it's a better way than how it has been traditionally done in the industry. I hope you know that as a potential investor, you deserve to be treated with respect. You're a business partner and you deserve to be treated like one. Most people, when I explain to them our way of doing business, are immediately on board. They understand why it makes more sense and they're ready to invest with us because we treat them with respect from day one.

I've said that the goal here is to get repeat investors and to keep doing new projects every year or so, and that's true. I am motivated for our clients to make money. We don't make money until they make money and the more money they make, the more money we make. We get a back-in after payout from the investor. This is the way my buddy David Moore set up his business and we are following suit. The reason I have been so successful with this new method of investing in oil and gas deals is because I am not afraid to get right out in front of people and talk to them; I explain what we're doing and how we're doing it and I ask them to come on board as partners.

If you're still on the fence about investing in oil and gas, either with King Operating or with another company that's doing business the same way, I would be happy to answer any questions you might have. It's important to me that when you have options about where to invest and what to do with your hard-earned money that you know the right questions to ask and that you feel confident that the people with whom you're entrusting your money are treating you honestly. I promise to take the time to answer your questions.

Now that you understand the Four Rs—returns, or whether the project makes economic sense; rate, or whether the project will produce high rates of oil and gas; running room, or the ability to have several locations; and repeatability, or the ability do it all over again—you should have a clearer concept of what a deal looks like that allows for maximum opportunity for making back your investment, and then some.

Once again, thank you for taking the time to read this book and for allowing me to show you a different—and, we believe, better— way of investing in oil and gas. I truly believe that if we work together as partners, there is no limit to what we can accomplish.

WORK WITH US

I f you would like to get in touch with me or with my team at King Operating, please do not hesitate to reach out. Our website, www.kingoperating.com, provides a list of our current offerings as well as an investor portal. Should you decide to invest with us, you will be able to see where your money is going and what it's being used for. The website also features a list of resources including recordings, videos, and a glossary to help you further understand some of the terminology you may encounter. Additionally, there is a whole section on tax benefits detailing the latest tax incentives and benefits available for oil and gas investments. You can also subscribe to our weekly email newsletter if you wish to be kept abreast of the progress of our current projects and any new deals on the horizon.

We can be reached directly at 214-420-3000. We are located in Dallas, Texas, at 6142 Campbell Road. There is a contact form on our website as well for general inquiries. If you have a more specific question, I can be reached at jyoung@kingoperating.com. I look forward to hearing from you.

THE JAY YOUNG SHOW

The Jay Young Show is a weekly podcast featuring insightful discussions with CEOs, entrepreneurs, authors, athletes, celebrities, and our military and veteran heroes from around the country. Each interview is a personal conversation that covers a wide range of topics from business, life lessons, successes, challenges, and everything in between.

Follow the show on Facebook Live each Thursday evening at 7pm CT.

www.thejayyoungshow.com

If you are interested in becoming a featured guest, please contact:

Kim Francis

kfrancis@thejayyoungshow.com

BIBLIOGRAPHY

American Oil & Gas Historical Society. "First Dry Hole." August 2018. https://aoghs.org/technology/first-dry-hole/.

Badenhausen, Kurt. "The NBA's Highest-Paid Players For 2018." *Forbes.* May 2018. https://www.forbes.com/sites/kurtbadenhausen/2018/02/07/the-nbas-highest-paid-players-on-and-off-the-court-for-2018/#3bb88b562853.

Baraniuk, Chris. "The Ghost Towns That Were Created by the Oil Rush." BBC. July 2016. http://www.bbc.com/future/story/20160715-the-ghost-towns-left-by-oil-booms-and-busts.

Baseball Almanac. "Year by Year Leaders for Batting Average." Accessed February 2019. http://www.baseball-almanac.com/hitting/hibavg3.shtml.

Baseball Reference. "Major League Baseball Batting Year-by-Year Averages." Accessed February 2019. https://www.baseball-reference.com/leagues/MLB/bat.shtml.

Blackmon, David. "Horizontal Drilling: A Technological Marvel Ignored." *Forbes*. January 2013. https://www.forbes.com/sites/davidblackmon/2013/01/28/horizontal-drilling-a-technological-marvel-ignored/.

Burrough, Bryan. *The Big Rich: The Rise and Fall of the Greatest Texas Oil Fortunes*. New York: Penguin Press, 2009.

Business Insider. "Crude Oil Price Today." Accessed February 2019. http://markets.businessinsider.com/commodities/oil-price?type=wti.

Carlson, Debbie. "The Best Stock Market Sectors in 2018." *U.S. News & World Report*. January 2018. https://money.usnews.com/investing/buy-and-hold-strategy/articles/2018-01-11/the-best-stock-market-sectors-in-2018.

Carter, Eric. "Should You Invest in Rental Real Estate?" *Forbes*. August 2017. https://www.forbes.com/sites/financialfinesse/2017/08/09/should-you-invest-in-rental-real-estate/#2cb5cfcb5c15.

Chamberlain, Alex. "A Key Overview of BP As a Company and Its Gulf of Mexico Accident." Market Realist. September 2019. https://marketrealist.com/2014/09/key-overview-bp-company-gulf-mexico-accident.

Chevron. "Seismic Imaging Technology." June 2018. https://www.chevron.com/stories/seismic-imaging.

Cluff, Jeremy. "NFL's Highest-Paid Offensive Linemen." *Arizona Central.* January 2017. https://www.azcentral.com/story/sports/heat-index/2017/01/06/nfls-highest-paid-offensive-linemen-2016-rankings/96246462/.

Cobb, Jeff. "The World Just Bought Its Two-Millionth Electric Car." HybridCARS. January 2017. https://www.hybridcars.com/the-world-just-bought-its-two-millionth-plug-in-car/.

Cussen, Mark. "Oil: A Big Investment with Big Tax Breaks." Investopedia. August 2018. https://www.investopedia.com/articles/07/oil-tax-break.asp.

Daily Reckoning. "Investing in Oil: A History." Accessed February 2019. https://dailyreckoning.com/investing-in-oil-a-history/.

DeMorro, Christopher. "Who Are Electric Car Buyers? Survey Says …" Clean Technica. May 2015. https://cleantechnica.com/2015/05/10/who-are-electric-car-buyers-survey-says/.

Econbrowser. "Oil prices as an indicator of global economic conditions." December 2014. http://econbrowser.com/archives/2014/12/oil-prices-as-an-indicator-of-global-economic-conditions.

Embassy of the United Arab Emirates. "The UAE and Global Oil Supply." Accessed February 2019. https://www.uae-embassy.org/about-uae/energy/uae-and-global-oil-supply.

Europa. "Global Trends in Renewable Energy Investment." April 2018. https://europa.eu/capacity4dev/unep/documents/ global-trends-renewable-energy-investment-2018.

Financial Industry Regulatory Authority. "The Reality of Investment Risk." Accessed February 2019. http://www.finra.org/ investors/reality-investment-risk.

Forbes. "Buying a House? Here Are 6 Reasons to Love a 20% Down Payment." February 2014. https://www.forbes.com/sites/ trulia/2014/02/26/buying-a-house-here-are-6-reasons-to-love-a-20-down-payment/#577e4f6949f8.

Geoprobe Systems. "Soil Vapor Sampling." Accessed February 2019. https://geoprobe.com/soil-vapor-sampling.

Gertner, Jon. "How They Lived – George Mitchell." *The New York Times.* December 2013. https://www.nytimes.com/news/ the-lives-they-lived/2013/12/21/george-mitchell/.

Goldman, David. "Ten Big Dot.com Flops." CNN. March 2010. http://money.cnn.com/galleries/2010/technology/1003/gallery. dot_com_busts/.

Greenhouse, Pat. "Are Long Baseball Contracts Worth It?" *Boston Globe.* April 2015. https://www.bostonglobe.com/ magazine/2015/04/01/are-long-baseball-contracts-worth/lJNSnC-mD8VjSvO9YQLb0zH/story.html.

Haile, Bartee. *Texas Boomtowns: A History of Blood and Oil.* South Carolina: The History Press, 2015.

http://geenergyfinancialservices.com/files/GE-EFS-Oil-Gas-Reserves-Deal-Preferences.pdf.

Kenton, Will. "Housing Bubble." Investopedia. April 2018. https://www.investopedia.com/terms/h/housing_bubble.asp.

Klippenstein, Matthew. "U.S. Vehicles Sales in H1 2017." Fleetcarma. September 2017. https://www.fleetcarma.com/electric-vehicle-sales-united-states-2017-half-year-update/).

Knightvest Management. "Company Overview." Accessed February 2019. https://knightvest.com/about/company-overview/.

Krome, Charles. "Car Depreciation: How Much Value Will a New Car Lose?" CarFax. November 2018. https://www.carfax.com/blog/car-depreciation.

LeDonne, Rob. "15 Worst Contrasts in Sports History." *Rolling Stone.* June 2018. https://www.rollingstone.com/sports/pictures/15-worst-contracts-in-sports-history-w489863/bobby-bonilla-new-york-mets-w489866.

Louidis, Nick K. "What Causes Oil Prices to Fluctuate?" Investopedia. April 2018. https://www.investopedia.com/ask/answers/012715/what-causes-oil-prices-fluctuate.asp.

Manfrenda, John. "The Real History of Fracking." OilPrice. April 2015. https://oilprice.com/Energy/Crude-Oil/The-Real-History-Of-Fracking.html.

McEwan, Mella. "Concho Agrees to Buy RSP in Permian Basin for $9.5 Billion." *Midland Reporter Telegram*. March 2018. https://www.mrt.com/business/oil/article/Concho-agrees-to-buy-RSP-Permian-for-9-5-billion-12789203.php.

Moskowitz, Peter "When Oil Boomtowns Go Bust." Vice. July 2016. https://www.vice.com/en_us/article/xdm854/when-oil-boomtowns-go-bust.

Murtaugh, Dan. "The Oil Ghost Towns of Texas." Bloomberg. September 2017. https://www.bloomberg.com/news/features/2017-09-26/the-oil-ghost-towns-of-texas.

North Dakota Oil. "A Brief History of North Dakota Oil Production." May 2011. https://northdakotaoil.wordpress.com/2011/05/14/the-start-of-horizontal-drilling-in-north-dakota-in-1987/.

OilScams.org. "A Historical Overview of Oil Investing." Accessed February 2019. http://www.oilscams.org/history-oil-investing.

OSHA. "Oil and Gas Extraction." Accessed February 2019. https://www.osha.gov/SLTC/oilgaswelldrilling/index.html.

Pallardy, Richard. "Deepwater Horizon Oil Spill of 2010." *Encyclopedia Britannica*. May 2016. https://www.britannica.com/event/Deepwater-Horizon-oil-spill-of-2010.

Patsy, Emily. "Callon Strengthens Midland Core With $327 Million Acquisition." Oil and Gas

Investor. September 2016. https://www.oilandgasinvestor.com/
callon-strengthens-midland-core-327-million-acquisition-1350421.

Quora. "How Do They Estimate The Amount of Oil
in an Oil Well?" March 2015. https://www.quora.com/
How-do-they-estimate-the-amount-of-oil-in-an-oil-well.

Railroad Commission of Texas Production Data Query System.
"Texas Permian Basin Oil Production 2008 through November
2018." February 2019. https://www.rrc.state.tx.us/media/41514/
permianbasin_oil_perday.pdf.

Railroad Commission of Texas. "Railroad Commission of Texas."
Accessed February 2019. http://www.rrc.state.tx.us/.

Rapier, Robert. "China's Oil Demand is Growing at More Than
Double Last Year's Pace."

Forbes. September 2017. https://www.forbes.com/sites/
rrapier/2017/09/18/chinas-oil-demand-is-growing-at-more-than-
double-last-years-pace/#2fe97b633ec0.

"Refining Technology Advances Focus on Reliability, Efficiency."
Oil & Gas Journal. March 2007. https://www.ogj.com/articles/
print/volume-105/issue-12/supplement-to-oil-gas-journal/
technology-forum-refining-equipment-services/refining-technology-
advances-focus-on-reliability-efficiency.html.

Reuters. "SM Energy to buy Permian Basin acreage for $1.6
billion." October 2016. https://www.reuters.com/article/us-sm-

energy-permian/sm-energy-to-buy-permian-basin-acreage-for-
1-6-billion-idUSKCN12I19T).

Right, Lawrence. "The Dark Bounty of Texas Oil." *The New Yorker*.
January 2018. https://www.newyorker.com/magazine/2018/01/01/
the-dark-bounty-of-texas-oil.

Rose & Associates LLP. "The Current Costs for Drilling a Shale
Well." Accessed February 2019. https://www.roseassoc.com/
the-current-costs-for-drilling-a-shale-well/.

Safire, William. "On Language; You Pays Yer Money." *The New
York Times*. February 1988. https://www.nytimes.com/1988/02/28/
magazine/on-language-you-pays-yer-money.html.

Scanlon, Bridget, et al. "Water Issues Related to Transitioning from
Conventional to Unconventional Oil Production in the Permian
Basin." *Environmental Science & Technology* 51, no. 18 (September
2017): 10903–10912. https://pubs.acs.org/doi/10.1021/acs.
est.7b02185.

Sharma, Rakesh. "OPEC vs. the U.S.: Who Controls Oil Prices?"
Investopedia. October 2018. https://www.investopedia.com/
articles/investing/081315/opec-vs-us-who-controls-oil-prices.asp.

Taylor, Alan. "The Alberta Tar Sands," *The Atlantic*.
September 2014. https://www.theatlantic.com/photo/2014/09/
the-alberta-tar-sands/100820/.

Taylor, Alan. "The Exxon Valdez Oil Spill: 25 Years Ago Today." *The Atlantic*. March 2014. https://www.theatlantic.com/photo/2014/03/the-exxon-valdez-oil-spill-25-years-ago-today/100703/.

TIGER 21. "The 1% is Cautiously Investing in Energy: TIGER 21 Chairman." December 2018. https://tiger21.com/1-cautiously-investing-energy-tiger-21-chairman.

Truong, Alice. "How Far Underground Are Oil Deposits?" HowStuffWorks. June 2018. https://science.howstuffworks.com/environmental/energy/underground-oil-deposits.htm.

U.S. Department of Energy. "Clean Energy." Accessed February 2019. https://www.energy.gov/science-innovation/clean-energy.

U.S. Department of Energy. "Liquefied Natural Gas." Accessed February 2019. https://www.energy.gov/fe/science-innovation/oil-gas/liquefied-natural-gas.

U.S. Energy Information Administration. "Natural Gas Explained." November 2018. https://www.eia.gov/energyexplained/index.php?page=natural_gas_use.

U.S. Energy Information Administration. "Nonrenewable Energy Explained." August 2018. https://www.eia.gov/energyexplained/?page=nonrenewable_home.

U.S. Energy Information Administration. "Renewable Energy Explained." July 2018. https://www.eia.gov/energyexplained/?page=renewable_home.

U.S. Energy Information Administration. "Short-Term Energy Outlook." February 2019. https://www.eia.gov/outlooks/steo/report/global_oil.php.

U.S. Energy Information Administration. "What Are Petroleum Products, and What Is Petroleum Used For?" April 2018. https://www.eia.gov/tools/faqs/faq.php?id=41&t=6.

Vlastelica, Ryan. "The Best Sector of This Bull Market Is the Greatest Investment Story Ever Told." Market Watch. March 2018. https://www.marketwatch.com/story/the-best-sector-of-this-bull-market-is-the-greatest-investment-story-ever-told-2018-03-08.

VOA. "Petroleum: A Short History of Black Gold." November 2007. https://learningenglish.voanews.com/a/a-23-2007-11-22-voa2-83131902/126857.html.

Walton, Justin. "The US States That Produce the Most Oil." Investopedia. October 2015. https://www.investopedia.com/articles/investing/100515/us-states-produce-most-oil.asp.

Waymarking. "The Grandin Well—Pennsylvania Historical Markers on Waymarking.com." Accessed February 2019. http://www.waymarking.com/waymarks/WM35YC_The_Grandin_Well.

White, Marian. "The Top 10 Largest U.S. Cities by Population." Moving.com. July 2019. https://www.moving.com/tips/the-top-10-largest-us-cities-by-population/.

Wikipedia. "Demographics of Houston." January 2019, https://en.wikipedia.org/wiki/Demographics_of_Houston.

Yergin, Daniel. *The Prize: The Epic Quest for Oil, Money & Power.* New York: Free Press, 2008.

A Special Offer from ForbesBooks

Other publications bring you business news. Subscribing to *Forbes* magazine brings you business knowledge and inspiration you can use to make your mark.

- Insights into important business, financial and social trends
- Profiles of companies and people transforming the business world
- Analysis of game-changing sectors like energy, technology and health care
- Strategies of high-performing entrepreneurs

Your future is in our pages.

To see your discount and subscribe go to Forbesmagazine.com/bookoffer.

Forbes